MW01201430

Women,
Words
& Wisdom

by

Solange Hertz

TUMBLAR HOUSE
' Bona Tempora Voluant'

Arcadia
MMXVI

Printed in the United States of America

ISBN 978-1-944339-01-2

Women, Words, & Wisdom

Visit our website at www.tumblarhouse.com

Nihil obstat: Edward A. Cerny, S.S., S.T.D.
Censor Librorum

Imprimatur: Francis P. Keough, D.D.
Archbishop of Baltimore
October 2, 1959

The *nihil obstat* and *imprimatur* are official declarations that a book or pamphlet is free of doctrinal and moral error. No implication is contained therein that those who have granted the *nihil obstat* and *imprimatur* agree with the opinions expressed.

Benedicite

Fly on the screen, praise the Lord,
Mouse in the attic, praise the Lord,
Child in the crib, praise the Lord,
Cat in the cradle, praise the Lord;
Ladybug, ladybug, praise the Lord,
Brown-eared puppydog, praise the Lord,
All Wisdom's little ones, praise the Lord!

First snow of winter, praise the Lord,
First spring jonquil, praise the Lord,
Apples for applesauce, praise the Lord,
Moles in the tulips, praise the Lord,
Jenny in the wrenhouse, praise the Lord,
Bird in the bush, praise the Lord,
Worms and aphids, praise the Lord,
Roses and ivy, berries and briar, praise the Lord,
Let all our garden praise the Lord!

Clock on the mantle made by man, praise the Lord,
Red geranium made by God, praise the Lord,
Beams and rafters, stones and floors, praise the Lord,
Beds and chairs and common table, praise the Lord,
Sheltering walls and creaking stairs, praise the Lord,
Wise books on the shelf, praise the Lord,
Foolish books on the shelf, praise the Lord,
Cake in the pan, praise the Lord,
Roast in the oven, praise the Lord,
Let things of the house all praise the Lord!

Head of the house, praise the Lord,
Wife and mother, praise the Lord,
Noisy children, praise the Lord;
Good St. Joseph, Mary most pure,
Guardian angels, saints in Heaven,
Angel of the House, help us praise the Lord!

Table of Contents

I. FIRST OF ALL

In spiritual books, there's one phrase that keeps popping up, in all languages: "I know a priest who," or "there was a servant of God who," followed by the description of some elevated experience. Unless the reader is a complete idiot—and therefore shouldn't be reading the book anyway—he knows that the author is now talking about *himself,* and is so terribly humble, he can't possibly admit that's who it is. Saints have done this. St. Teresa many times "knew a nun who," for saints are really humble, but I'm sure they didn't mean to set a style.

I've read a lot of these books, and was just about to begin this one with "I know a housewife who often does her ironing wishing she owned the complete works of Tertullian." But let's not fool around. You would know perfectly well that the housewife is little ole me. This is a personal book, not because I want it to be, but because I'm a woman and can't write any other kind. If I started a commentary on St. Thomas Aquinas it would undoubtedly degenerate into what my children think of him, what questions I expect him to clarify for me in heaven and what essence and existence mean as applied to geraniums. Furthermore, if you think the situations and characters herein depicted are "purely fictitious and bear no resemblance, etc.," well, I can only say that's a pretty silly thing to say about any book.

I don't want to write this at all. As far as I know, my motives are purely cathartic, in the highest Greek sense. I'm writing because I just can't help it. For four years I figured this urge was a diabolic temptation to sneak out of my humdrum lot. In desperation, I trapped two Trappists in their own visitors' parlor and asked them point-blank how you tell a terrible temptation from an inspiration.

"Search us," they said cheerily. "It's a problem we struggle with all the time."

"But I have this horrible compulsion to write a book," I confided shamefacedly.

"Well then, why don't you?" they asked.

An answer like this springs from Holy Simplicity, which takes years of virtue to acquire. Never would it have occurred to me to cut the Gordian knot like that.

"Whatever you write, though," they suggested, "please keep it light. The world is full of dull books."

I'll try.

Certainly if writing under difficulty produces great books, this one will be a humdinger. Though I'm not faced with the prospect of burning my own hair for warmth in a cold garret while my numbed fingers stumble across a re-used sheet of paper in a race to the death with creditors, I have other problems just as good in maintaining creative tensions: a husband and five children who expect to be fed at *all* the appointed times; a little terror who creeps out of the playpen into the wastebasket and chews the discarded typewriter ribbon; a female teenager who said (and I quote), "You're going to write a book! Well, if you can, I can!" and has set to with a leaky pen upstairs; also, two horses who spend their days—and nights—inventing daring escapes out of our pasture into the neighbor's tulip beds; a faulty water pump which must be kicked in zero weather; and our phone rings just as much as other people's.

"Oh, blessed inconvenience!" as St. Mary Magdalen Postel would no doubt say. What untapped wealth of grace and virtue! I simply can't let this opportunity slip by me. Despite all these odds—and I'm sure you'll agree they're odd—I've *got* to write a book.

You've heard of a comedian's comedian? Well, I guess I'm setting myself up as a housewife's housewife. That's who's writing it, and that's whom it's for. I've picked the biggest subject and the biggest reading public I could think of. There are millions of us. And one of us just happens to be the Queen of Heaven, of angels, prophets, martyrs, confessors, and the Mother of God Himself!

Writing about housewives can begin anywhere, lead anywhere, and end never. Keeping to the subject is going to be easy because it covers everything, all knowledge, all human experience. Any science, attitude, talent or virtue can serve the housewife in her myriad roles. Can a being whose whole function is the extension and nourishment of society ever have too much food in the cupboard?

One adornment I've always felt I could safely do without is higher mathematics. Well, I have a son studying it now, and the other day he asked, "Mother, how do you visualize the square of a minus number?" I came clean and admitted I couldn't, but not without some sense of failure, like Old Mother Hubbard when she couldn't produce that bone.

Let me tell you, if I heard that one of you out there was studying cuneiform inscriptions or well drilling while the wash soaks, I'd cheer you on. They're bound to come in handy one of these days. I once picked up in the Library of Congress a pamphlet on chair caning written for the instruction of the feeble-minded in a useful trade, and I've been replacing chair seats around the house ever since. Do you know where I can get one on juggling? (Our stairs here are very narrow.)

But this is all incidental. The subject goes much deeper, as we all know. One stupendous fact stands out above all others, and it is this: When God chose a co-redemptrix to aid His beloved Son in the salvation of mankind, he could have picked a lady statistician, or a prophetess, a cook, a teacher, a charwoman, or Molly Pitcher. He could have picked a seamstress, a nurse, a woman philosopher or a bank clerk. But He didn't. He picked all of them. He picked a housewife.

She is Mary Immaculate, a laywoman and a daughter of Eve. He made her the channel of all the grace He pours into our fallen world—the astounding grace of redemption, of priesthood, of martyrdom, and every actual grace leading the lowliest sinner to Him.

This holy housewife is given to us not only as our spiritual mother, but as our model. An awesome thought! We can never imitate her at all unless we imitate her in her fundamental role —the mainspring of her sanctity—her role as a channel of grace. Every woman comes into the world to transmit life, supernatural or physical. Sometimes she is relieved of the duty of transmitting physical life, but of spiritual life, never. This is what I think about when the teakettle whistles or the children burst in the front door, and I repeat, it's an awesome thought.

We call Mary "Spiritual vessel, Vessel of honor, Vessel of singular devotion, House of gold, Ark of the Covenant," because a woman must contain. In spite of herself, she gives what she contains.

Mary, who contained God, composed for us a very beautiful piece called The Magnificat. It's very feminine, very personal, and was produced without its interfering with the performance of any of her homely duties. I therefore humbly dedicate this little effort to her, put together as it is between the marketing and the washing, Holy Mass and the oven.

Ave, Maria, Gate of Heaven and Queen of Housewives, please: a blessing!

II. THE MOST

I'm dedicating this book to the Blessed Virgin most of all because it's a vulgar book, written for vulgar people, and the Blessed Virgin is the most vulgar of all saints. If you think this is blasphemy, just wait a minute while I reach for my Latin dictionary, an item no housewife should ever be without.

It says here, "*Vulgus*, noun, neuter," and the following meanings are listed: the people, the great multitude, the public. It doesn't say low-down, good-for-nothing people. It just says a lot of them. A little farther up the page I see the verb vulgare. It means "to make common to all, to communicate, make accessible to all." Understandably enough, a secondary meaning is "to publish a book."

So, I repeat, this is a vulgar book. I'm vulgar, I'm vulgarizing, and I'm dedicating this book to the most vulgar of all saints. Our Blessed Lady is vulgar in the same sense that the Catholic Church is vulgar. She's for everybody, everywhere. She's vulgar as the Bible is vulgar, which, incidentally, was called the Vulgate long before printing was invented.

Our Lady is the most universal and encompassing of all God's creatures. Her vulgarity makes angels gasp and men marvel. Whatever unbelievers may say about her, there's one thing they can't deny: her outstanding ability to draw crowds. At Lourdes, at Fatima, at school May Days, at Marian celebrations of any kind, there's always a crowd if a crowd can be had—a real, great big *vulgus*. She specifically told little St. Bernadette and the three Portuguese children that she wanted lots of people to come to her shrines, and come they do!

She doesn't despise us just because there happen to be a lot of us. Our word vulgar has come to have the terrible overtones it has simply because we are sinful and proud and rate our scale of values on degree of scarcity. "What there's a lot of can't be worth anything" is what we now mean by vulgar, and a woman who says

5

she's "just a housewife" has fallen without a fight into this way of thinking.

For some reason, we also think that when there's a lot of some things, it naturally follows that they're all the same, all alike. In these days of assembly line mentality, even children think this way although they of all people should certainly know better. Maybe it's not just the assembly line. Maybe it's one of the effects of original sin.

I remember floundering around to find some way of keeping my two younger boys occupied one afternoon when they seemed particularly bent on destroying each other. Luckily, we live near a sizable woods.

"Look, boys, tell you what!" I beamed desperately. "You go out into the woods and find me two leaves exactly alike, and I'll give you five whole dollars!"

The look on their faces was something to behold, because mother, while not exactly tight, isn't one to throw cash around, especially in their direction.

"Are you serious?" Tavy asked. (He's older.)

When I nodded, he was off like a rocket, with his brother at his heels, both of them intent on making a monkey out of mother in five minutes. They came back almost immediately with a fistful of leaves all "just alike." But when they were made to look at them more closely, all sorts of unaccountable little variations began to appear. After several more dashes into the woods, growing progressively less enthusiastic, they gave up, the five dollars finally evaporating from their dreams.

I felt like a heel, but the wonderment has never left them. It could have been sea shells, pebbles, bugs, flowers, sticks, clouds, almost anything that looks "all alike" until you really look.

It could have been souls, if we could see souls. St. John of the Cross said that in all his experience as a director of souls, he never came across two who were alike "by so much as by half." When you consider that faith tells us that one human soul is a greater creation than all the material universe, you begin to get a faint idea of what it is the Blessed Virgin sees in crowds.

She herself always had a particular talent for disappearing into them. The first time Scripture mentions her, it describes her simply as a girl betrothed to a man named Joseph and adds almost as an afterthought, "the girl's name was Mary." Mary, or Miriam, was probably the most common or "vulgar" name possible to a Jewish girl in her day. Scholars don't even agree on its meaning, but many incline to the view that it means only "lady," a label which could be applied to any girl. Ultimately, she stood at the foot of the Cross with two other Marys, Mary Magdalene and Mary Cleophas, always one among others.

So it seems hardly fortuitous that the only recorded words of human praise given to her during her lifetime were spoken by a "certain woman from the crowd," who shouted in our Lord's direction, "Blessed is the womb that bore thee, and the breasts that nursed thee!" *(Luke 11:27)*. The Gospel doesn't even mention her name, but she could easily have been you or I.

The Blessed Virgin is vulgar, because she is every woman, and exemplifies in her life all the states possible to a woman: a child, a virgin, a wife, a mother, and finally, a widow. She is everywhere at once and reflects perfectly in a creaturely way the omnipresence of God, Who is so hard to see because He is so obvious.

Father Gerard Manley Hopkins wrote what I think is a most beautiful poem about this quality of hers. Being a poet, he didn't call her vulgar. He calls his poem "The Blessed Virgin Compared to the Air We Breathe," and said we "are meant to share/Her life as life does air." What is so necessary, so unremarkable as air! But Father Hopkins wasn't indulging in fantasy. Like all good poets, he was stating fact. We not only share her life; she insists on sharing ours.

I got a solid demonstration of this once in a leper colony, of all places. (Don't be surprised. Housewives are like mice. They can turn up anywhere.) I took my daughter Lydia with me, for though I may not provide her lessons in tap dancing or the bass viol, I do take her to leprosaria when occasion offers. (Oh, no, I'm not! Leprosy is very hard to catch, even harder than T.B.)

We went because I was just plain curious, with no philanthropic motives whatever to my credit. I just wanted to see the disease our Lord cured so many times, the "white death" the Church Fathers claim most exemplifies the ravages of sin on the soul.

Recovering from her surprise at learning we were Americans (we have a reputation the world over for being terrified of germs), the head nurse took us to meet the priest attached to this leper colony. I explained to him I was just plain curious and that Lydia didn't really want to come, and he accepted that.

I learned later that he had a great reputation for sanctity "even in his own Order" —the acid test among religious, I'm told. He was not only reputed to multiply rice most inexplicably for the colony's denizens, but he was also reported given to performing all sorts of odd little miracles just to be nice. The one that impressed me most was the time he was supposed to have produced peaches in the midst of the banana belt to please a dying leper who had never seen peaches, but wanted some. He got them before the man died—not fresh peaches, however. Any ordinary saint can do that, I was informed. Father produced *canned* ones, which is what the leper wanted.

It was no surprise to me that the said Father had an extraordinary devotion to our Lady. While he was showing me around the colony, he stopped dead still before a large-as-life statue of her which was standing in a corner of one of the school buildings.

"Isn't she beautiful?" he asked, looking at us narrowly.

It was a bad moment. Lydia and I didn't dare look at each other. The statue was namby-pamby plaster, in the style of what we in the bosom of the family call "Hoover Administration Baroque." To make matters worse, the paint was peeling badly, and there were large white patches of plaster showing through on her hands and face.

I took refuge in "holy equivocation." "Yes," I said, "she is beautiful," meaning our Lady, not the statue.

Father seemed satisfied. "You know," he said, "I'm glad you like her. I was just about to send her off to be repainted a while back, but I didn't."

We were politely silent.

"I'll tell you why I didn't. The day before she was to go, I came on one of my patients [he never called them lepers] praying here in front of her. Do you know what he told me?"

We didn't.

"Well, he turned to me and pointed to the white spots on the statue, and he said, 'Look, Father, the Blessed Mother has become one of us!' After that, you know, I just had to let her be."

Lydia and I still couldn't look at each other, but for a different reason. We should have seen the resemblance immediately. We had just passed wards and wards, huts and huts of lepers, and could understand only too well why the good Father had to "let her be." According to last count, there are anywhere from three to five million lepers in our world.

That's how vulgar the Blessed Virgin can get. Isn't she THE MOST?

III. HI. ANNA

"*Pauperem e stercore attollit*," I often pray. Freely translated, this can mean "God will eventually raise a poor woman up from those endless diapers."

It's hardly coincidence that this verse first occurs on the lips of a housewife some 3000 years ago, and things haven't changed much in all that time. Essentials are essentials; and they make up most of the domestic day.

Under the inspiration of the Holy Spirit a woman called Anna prayed before the Tabernacle at Silo—long before the Temple was built in Jerusalem—and gave forth her now famous Canticle, which is part of Holy Scripture and is chanted solemnly by the Church all over the world in the Divine Office. When Anna uttered it, she was thanking God, much as did the Blessed Virgin in the Magnificat, for the grace of motherhood.

Anna's life had been far from happy. Besides all the cooking and cleaning, mending and washing common to women in a household, she had a special trial the law now spares most of us: she had to share her husband, Elcana. He had another wife, whose name was Phenenna.

Phenenna's character can be easily deduced by any woman reading between the lines of the story as it appears in First Samuel. If she were living today, she would probably be the loudest at the PTA, an oracle of strong-minded solutions to other people's problems—all sensible and incontestable, and she most likely had that dastardly faculty of always doing exactly as she pleased about everything by insisting that Duty forced her to it. Everything she did was maddeningly right. Her soufflés rarely fell. She could stay on key effortlessly and tunelessly, and always knew all the verses. She was a demon housekeeper and had labels on all jars and boxes.

She probably drove Elcana to quiet desperation, but he could never in conscience object to anything she did, because it was always so blatantly RIGHT. He didn't like her, and being a just and pious man, he felt rather sheepish and guilty about it. Scripture understates his attitude eloquently by simply saying, "He loved *Anna*."

Consequently, he tried to make this up to Phenenna in small ways, and ended by giving in to her in all major household decisions, lest he be forced to accuse himself of allowing pique to influence his exercise of authority. You can imagine how Phenenna thrived on this.

Poor Anna was the Cinderella of the ménage, a quiet, contemplative sort. It is true that like all contemplatives she had the better part, in this case her husband's love; but again, like most contemplatives, she had little she could point to in the way of solid achievement to justify her existence. She didn't even have any children, a most terrible reproach among the Israelites.

Phenenna, of course, had oodles of them, and never tired of rubbing it in. Had there been photographers then, she would have had a large family group picture placed where Elcana and the friends he brought to dinner couldn't miss it. In company, she probably dwelt on "woman's highest duty" and the satisfactions of woman's life "full lived" as she waited for Anna to clear the table between courses and quiet the last baby.

"Anna has so much more free time than I do," she would have told the bridge club, adding in dulcet tones, "because of course she hasn't any children." This supposedly proved even God had no use for Anna. This being the case, we can be sure Anna was given more than her share of the housework, not to mention cleaning up Phenenna's children.

Anna suffered silently, except when Phenenna reduced her to tears, to the point, Scripture tells us, that she couldn't eat. She was probably always in such a state of nerves she often dropped things, making herself look pretty incompetent on any level. Even Elcana, who loved her, couldn't seriously find much reason to praise her that anyone would understand. Maybe she wasn't even pretty. Besides, those tears and that runny nose got him down.

Anna's suffering as the Holy Spirit reveals it to us was rather the quintessence of the housewife's: endless little pinpricks on the personal level, a round of humiliating little chores, little misunderstandings, little messes to clean up—nothing big, just devastatingly unremitting.

Anna's only hope was the hope of the hopeless: God. We are told that once when the family went on its accustomed pilgrimage to Silo, Phenenna had been particularly obnoxious. Before the Tabernacle, Anna,

> ...had her heart full of grief, she prayed to the Lord, shedding many tears... And she made a vow, saying: O Lord of hosts, if thou wilt look down on the affliction of thy servant, and wilt be mindful of me, and not forget thy handmaid, and wilt give to thy servant a man child: I will give him to the Lord all the days of his life, and no razor shall come upon his head *(I Kings 1:10-11)*.

Then came the final insult. Her prayer was so fervent and so interior ("her voice was not heard at all"), the priest who had been watching her walked up and accused her of being drunk. This priest, incidentally, was Heli. He was very good at his job and good at criticizing others, but he let his two sons go to pot. God eventually punished him, but as is His wont, He crowned Anna's sorrow and humiliation most gloriously. She became the mother of the prophet Samuel. Not even the names of Phenenna's children are considered worthy of mention.

When Samuel was weaned and brought to the Tabernacle to be left there in God's service as his mother had promised, Anna's soul overflowed into the majestic Canticle which bears her name. She begins, "My heart hath rejoiced in the Lord, and my horn is exalted in my God: my mouth is enlarged over my enemies: because I have joyed in thy salvation" *(I Kings 2:1)*.

How many of Phenenna's petty persecutions lie buried in those words? And in the following:

> There is none holy as the Lord is: for there is no other beside thee, and there is none strong like our God. Do not multiply to speak lofty things, boasting: let old matters depart from your mouth. For the Lord is a God of all knowledge, and to Him are thoughts prepared. The bow of the mighty is overcome: and the weak are girt with strength. They that were full before have hired out themselves for bread: and the hungry are filled; so that the barren hath borne many *(I Kings 2:2-5)*.

Anna was blessed with three more sons and two daughters after Samuel as a reward for consecrating him to God; "and she that had many children is weakened" *(I Kings 2:5)*.

Oh Phenenna! We can't help wondering what happened to her.

"The Lord killeth and maketh alive: He bringeth down to hell and bringeth back again. The Lord maketh poor and maketh rich: He humbleth and He exalteth." *(I Kings 2:6-7)*.

The similarity between Anna's Canticle and the Magnificat is very striking and has often been commented on. Both praise God for his loving care and special concern for the lowly and unnoticed. I'll not risk tangling with biblical experts by going into the question of whether or not Anna actually composed her Canticle, or trying to explain how it is that verse eight occurs almost verbatim in one of David's psalms. It satisfies me to know that pious Jews never claimed originality in their praise of God. Expressive, solid phrases were used over and over again without fear of plagiarism whenever they happened to suit.

If Anna didn't compose her Canticle, all I can say is that the author or editor who put it in her mouth was a sound psychologist. For me, she utters it quite spontaneously as it appears in the text. I don't mean, however, that its composition was spontaneous, any more than what I am writing now is being composed now. Writing takes hours; what one writes takes years.

In Anna's case, her effort could only have been the fruit of a deep interior life, developed in much quiet suffering and naked cleaving to God. Nor do I mean that all this interior suffering and prayer, ultimately breaking into splendid joy, were Anna's. Her Canticle has generations of authors, beginning with Adam's wife. Some of the authors were known as Sarah, Rebecca, or Rachel, but most of them were unknown. They have to be unknown and of little consequence because that's the point of the whole song. Anna just happens to have gathered it all up and thrown it like a big bouquet to those who followed after—to Ruth perhaps, to Elizabeth, to Mary, to me and to every mother who ever scrubbed a floor.

This brings me back to *pauperem e stercore attollit*, the next verse, which begins, "He raiseth up the needy from the dust, and lifteth up the poor from the dunghill" *(I Kings 2:8)*. It is the very verse which was incorporated into David's psalm. The vast majority of exegetes, being men, can't know the chords these lines strike in a housewife's heart—especially in the Latin, which is much more graphic.

I don't know whether in the original Hebrew it's possible to tell whether a man or a woman is "the needy" and "the poor," but I know what Anna had in mind all right. This verse sums up in a nutshell one of the housewife's major problems: *How to support God's action in her regard by supernaturalizing her constant contact with physical dirt and make it serve her supernatural end.*

For it must be borne in mind that God raises the poor and needy from the dust and the dunghill in order "that he may sit with princes, and hold the throne of glory" *(I Kings 2:8).*

It is not considered good taste for a homemaker to call attention to the fact that she is occupied for a great part of her day in the removal or elimination of filth, only the means varying with her economic status. If she keeps bringing it up in conversation, her less conscientious sisters may accuse her of entertaining a guilt complex which she is compulsively scouring away, Lady Macbeth style. At best she'll be accused of sordid thinking, of self-pity, of not being able to see the home because of the house.

Let's be vulgar. Any housewife who seriously tries to banish the thought of dirt from her thinking might as well try to banish dirt. Pretending it isn't there or isn't important may well leave her a schizophrenic in never-never land, with a calm sweet smile covering a vacuous brain, power-thinking she's Marie Antoinette. She might as well try to pursue virtue by dismissing all thought of sin.

So let's call a spade a spade, or a mop a mop. Dirt and filth are a part—and even a very large part of our existence. I can produce my vacuum cleaner, a dish washer, a washing machine, several hundred feet of plumbing, brooms, scouring powders, soaps, shampoos, disinfectants, toothbrushes, clothespins, steel wool, doormats, sponges, washcloths and a whole bag full of rags to prove my point. I'm in intimate contact with all.

This is a humiliating fact to face and no doubt accounts for the booming sale of satin lounging pajamas and filmy housecoats. Lots of us like to pretend we don't *really* have to submit to it, that when we do it's only out of the goodness of our hearts and our sporting blood. Refusal to admit that scrubbing is an integral part of the average woman's life is pure pride. It's the real reason the new bride can be driven to quiet fury when she sees her husband relaxing happily with the paper while she does the dishes. *His* dishes! She may rebel by deliberately leaving them in the sink until morning. Then, of course, it's worse. She has added open rebellion to pride. Husband goes to the office, and she's left to grope alone for the satisfactions of her high vocation as best she can.

Dirty dishes, dirty diapers, dusty floors, unwashed bodies, smeared woodwork, vomit, soiled clothes and dandruff are quite simply effects of Eve's fall and must be accepted as such. In these physical aspects God keeps before our eyes the hideousness of sin. Leaving aside its obvious value as a penance, our battle against dirt, our repugnance for it, is a symbolic battle against sin. The girls who accuse the wizard housekeeper of a guilt complex are on very solid ground. The line between the garbage can and the confessional is rather fine, as any priest can tell you. Actually, the housewife's daily unremitting warfare with dirt is very like a parish priest's warfare against sin—a thought most deftly developed by Bernanos in a speech he puts into the mouth of his crusty old Curé de Torey in the *Diary of a Country Priest*.

He begins by telling the young curate,

> …we say the Church is the Bride of Christ. What's a wife, lad—a real woman as a man'd hope to get if he's fool enough not to follow the advice of Saint Paul? … I'll tell you: it's a sturdy gal who's not afraid of work, but who knows the way of things, that everything has to be done over and over again, until the end.

If we pursue the Curé's analogy, we see the housewife performs on the natural plane what the Church performs on the supernatural plane. The removal of dirt is, however, more than symbolic. It's sacramental. This means that with sufficient faith and the proper intentions, it can to some measure effect what it signifies. It is *de fide* that all of material creation is a sign of spiritual reality, a pale temporary image of something else far more real than anything we can see, feel or imagine, and that by contact with the material we are meant to be drawn to the eternal. This means it should lead us to God.

Does it follow that a housewife in the state of grace can battle sin by battling dirt? Certainly. This simple thought is staggering in its implications and practical applications. When a soul united to God in love scours the sink she performs a supernatural act, an act which is expiatory, redemptive. At the same time she is practicing humility, charity, obedience—a whole host of virtues.

Not to be overlooked is the fact that most of the dirt she cleans isn't her own, but of others' making: others' muddy shoes track up the floor; others' dishes clutter the table. Let this remind her she is a member of the Mystical Body of Christ, and that He came to earth to take others' sins upon Himself. No one living with His life can contend with only *her* dirt, *her* sins. Oh, no! We're all in this together. It's *our* dirt, *our* sins! It's the housewife's special little share in the Redemption to be able to atone for others' sins by washing others' clothes.

It's a quiet share, with no human glory in it, but Anna accepted it. The Blessed Virgin, who "wrapped Him in swaddling clothes," accepted it. Now they "sit with princes, and hold the throne of glory" *(I Kings 2:8)*, because eventually God raises the housewife from her dustpan and those diapers!

IV. MEDITATION IN A DUSTPAN

My husband says I shouldn't write so much about dirt. (He's a man.) Actually, dirt isn't just a penance. It's a higher education. Dirt is to a housekeeper what heresy is to the Church. It's something to beat against, learn from, and grow strong on. I've learned more from just looking at dirt than any man could possibly imagine.

I suspect I'm not alone in this, but you can't get many people to admit it. One shining exception was a housewife like myself who lived next door to me back in the early days of my marriage when we lived in suburbia. During the coffee break one morning, with our babies stashed dry in the playpen, she invited me to speculate with her, in a scientific spirit, on the precise point at which good food (which may have required hours of artistic preparation) became GARBAGE. There ensued something like the following:

"Does it happen the minute your husband positively refuses to eat it?"

"No, I guess it's when you get up from the table and leave it to itself on the plate."

"Suppose you went back and finished it later? Would you be eating garbage?"

"Then I guess it's when it's scraped together with all the other leftovers."

"Is it being mixed up that does it? What about tossed salads? They're mixed up, but not garbage."

"Maybe when you set it out for the dog?"

"Who would ever admit feeding his dog garbage! You call *that* scraps!"

"But is it *really* garbage?"

"Well, it's certainly garbage when you put it in the garbage can!"

"What would you be putting it in the garbage can for if it wasn't already garbage?"

"What is garbage? Seems to me we have to settle the definition first, before we can even begin to talk about it."

We never solved the problem. I guess trouble in the playpen prevented it. I for one couldn't have solved it anyway, because I didn't believe in God at the time. As St. Anselm put it, "*Credo ut intelligam*:" You have to have the faith before you can reason anything out all the way.

Nevertheless, I offer this conversation as proof positive that speculative thinking on the philosophical level does go on in suburbs. It's hidden, but there.

Practical repercussions in this case were negligible, unless it contributed in some mysterious way to one of our family's most solid traditions: my weekly *soupe garbage*, pronounced *garbahge* in deference to my French blood and the inevitable onion. Into this culinary triumph all unmanageable leftovers disappear to be transformed into something rich and strange, more or less delicious, as the ingredients would have it.

I mention it because it's the only instance I can cite offhand where garbage (in its broadest sense, of course) can be said to become good food again (also in its broadest sense). Though it's never theoretically impossible, it's rather like unboiling the egg. To me my *soupe* has become a symbol of Redemption. The family can't always see it that way, but I derive much consolation from the thought as I watch it bubble on the stove.

I hadn't thought about the old garbage discussion for years until the other day. I was sweeping the kitchen floor and had just cajoled all the sweepings into the dustpan. For some reason I was drawn to examine them very carefully.

This isn't recommended behavior. If any friend had come in at the moment and found me squatting chin in hand a few inches above the floor, peering into my dustpan for almost a quarter of an hour, I suppose my husband would have caught it for making me live so long "isolated out there in the middle of the country."

What I saw was positively fascinating. Crumpled eggshells. Lots of red brick dust from the brick floor. The bricks used to be the second storey of the old North Fork Baptist Church out our way. When the roof blew off the third time some years back, the congregation decided to face facts and bring the building down to just one level. We bought the surplus bricks for a penny apiece and laid them out in the kitchen. This allows me to trample heresy as I prepare dinner.

But, to continue: Well-covered with brick dust was an old dry tomato skin. Then a greasy marble. Several corn flakes. Lint from the dryer. Two crumpled paper napkins. A crust of toast with jelly (wineberry, from our own bushes) on it. Several pieces of broken glass. A rubber band and, as they say in the ads for country auctions, "other articles too numerous to mention." (Oh, yes, I sweep every day.)

Looked at dispassionately, each of these items was in itself quite unobjectionable—a "good" as scholastic philosophy would put it. An eggshell is an eggshell. No one, surely, will dispute that. On the egg it's especially proper, useful, a perfect ceramic and one of God's minor masterpieces. Who can find brick dust unworthy, especially in bricks, or back in its native clay? Or in the Baptist Church? (I'm not indifferent, just tolerant.) A tomato skin on a tomato is beautiful. A marble is a marble, a miracle of the glassmaker's art. The grease on it, back in the grease can or the hog, is dandy.

So mentally putting the corn flakes back in their box, the lint back on the clothes and the rubber band all the way to the rubber plantation, I couldn't find any dirt. Then what was it that made this mixture of good things so revolting? Even the invisible germs were perfectly good in their place.

That was when I remembered the garbage conversation. It must have been perseverating for fully fifteen years. So that was what St. Thomas Aquinas meant when he postulated evil has no real existence! That all things in themselves are essentially good. No wonder we couldn't find out what makes garbage garbage. We were trying to solve what St. Paul was content to call "the mystery of iniquity."

Evil exists only because good exists. If good disappeared, evil would disappear, because evil is simply a principle of disorder—a perversion of God's perfect creatures from their proper uses and ends. No wonder after I got through imagining all the contents of the dustpan into their proper places the "dirt" was gone and the dustpan empty. What's more my sweeping, oh joy, had become needless.

When I finished applying the same technique to the activities and passions of mankind, avarice had turned back into justice and economy, love of self into love of God, anger into zeal, lies were straightened out into truth, and lust into the service of creation. Hell was turned into Heaven. Jails, insane asylums, hospitals, battleships and brothels were as empty as my dustpan. The world was as God meant it to be.

Maybe you've always known this. I haven't. Oh, I guess I knew it intellectually, but I never really knew it and possessed it until I saw it in the dustpan. All the sins of the world are there.

As I said, there's a lot to be learned from just looking at dirt and sweeping it up. And how a housewife hopes to get by without Thomistic philosophy, I can't imagine.

V. SOME GOOD MUTTERS

As the gambler said, "I know it's crooked, but it's the only game in town!"

A housewife may not particularly want to be holy, but what else on earth is there for her to do? In itself, a duller and more pointless existence than hers can't be imagined—unless she's headed for Heaven. And she's got to head for Heaven, because no housewife in her right mind would want worse than she's got already, in the other place.

I'm not mentioning Purgatory, because the way I see it, deliberately shooting for Purgatory is an insult to Almighty God. It's a fine place for people who aim high and miss, but as a target, it has nothing whatever to recommend it.

Our Lord said very clearly, "You therefore are to be perfect, even as your heavenly Father is perfect" *(Matt. 5:48)*, which is such an outrageous command on the face of it, that if we hadn't gotten used to hearing it, we could hardly stand it. He didn't say this, moreover, to a select little coterie in a small room. The Gospel tells us He said it to a *crowd* (the *vulgus* again) out in the open, for anybody who cared to listen.

There being little choice in the matter, as the gambler said, we might as well settle down to winning the game, if possible. And the game really is crooked. God stacks the deck in our favor to a degree few gamblers would dream of. Didn't He say, "I am the God of Jacob"? Jacob means *cheater* in Hebrew. And we know he certainly played to win! When you bet on a sure thing, you put every cent you've got in the pot. You even borrow what you can. You make side bets. Any gambler can tell you that.

First of all, I understand you have to have a slogan, some little catchphrase that will cheer you up and keep you playing when you don't seem to be getting the cards. Our encyclopedia says a slogan is "a word or phrase designed to persuade people to take some

21

action." It must work. "Tippecanoe and Tyler too" certainly elected Tyler all right.

Of course dignified people don't have slogans. They have "mottoes." Why a motto is more uppity, I don't know. The word comes from the corrupted Latin *muttum*, which means mutter or grunt. It is presumably something you gasp out in desperation when the going gets really rough, like Sir Jacob Astly before' going into battle: "Lord, I'll probably forget You, but don't You forget me!" So it really doesn't matter whether you call it slogan or motto. Just have one!

Popes, bishops, abbots and other prelates, who often have a very rough time of it, choose a motto suitable for their coats-of-arms, or devices, when they are elevated to office. It is meant to set the general tone of what they hope to accomplish. St. Pius X chose "To Restore All Things in Christ." My Bishop, who has a great devotion to our Lady, chose *Per Matrem Dei*. St. Ignatius picked out *Ad Majorem Dei Gloriam*—For the Greater Glory of God—when he founded his Society. St. Francis de Sales liked *Vive Jésus*! St. Joan settled all her problems with *Dieu le Veut*—God Wills It—because that settles anything.

These were of course made public, which adds an extra incentive to living up to them, but they don't have to be. As a matter of fact, I learn that private mottoes change right along as one progresses in the spiritual life and one's views enlarge. Sister Elizabeth of the Trinity began with *Agenda Contra* while she was still fighting hard against external failings, then worked through "God in me and I in Him" before arriving at the pinnacle of the *Laudem Gloriae* by which she is known, God's Praise of Glory.

Janet Erskine Stuart, a great Mother General of the Society of the Sacred Heart, thought up oodles of good mottoes. One was taken from a poem about a sinking ship:

> As the screws said to the rivets,
> "In case of doubt, HOLD ON!"

This is a peachy one, I think, a real *muttum*, comparable in its lowly way to the Church's "*Domine, ad adjuvandum me festina!*[1]"

---

[1] "O Lord, make haste to help me."

It's good for anything from a wobbling vocation to soap in your eyes.

It's best to start small. A crony of mine decided on "*Sursum Corda!*[2]" It has dignity and can be said quickly. It seems to cheer her up on blue Mondays. Frankly, I had some trouble settling on one. Though I liked the gambler's, it somehow didn't seem quite personal enough. I thought about "Don't give up the ship!" but that sounded as if I were in command of something.

Everybody tells me what I need first of all in the spiritual life is humility, and I found just what I wanted eventually. It was in the comics. It's "I yam what I yam and tha's all that I yam, I yam Popeye the Sailor Man!" Don't sneer. This is a very good spiritual slogan, quite untranslatable into Latin. It has all sorts of overtones and possibilities: "I yam what I yam, I yamma housewife who does the ironing wishing she owned the works of Tertullian," or "I yam what I yam and I'd better do something about it." Oh, it's limitless.

Popeye himself as an inspiration is no slouch. He is what he is. First of all, he's a creature and admits it. It's not "I am Who am," like God, Who is pure Being. It's "I yam *what* I yam." I yamma creature. What that means in his case is being pretty homely and spindly, a simple seaman with no privileges of rank and little control of the ship, but with a strong sense of mission. Every good that Popeye accomplishes he does purely by virtue of spinach, a strengthening green cordially detested by many. With this spinach in him, however, he sallies forth and tackles bullies several times his size and pulverizes them with his "fisks." (Obviously, he can't even speak good English.)

He is what he is, no airs, no illusions; he eats his spinach (does God's Will); and proceeds to give battle to his enemies (the world, the flesh and the devil). It's the life of the Christian in a nutshell. Really, I like Popeye's attitude. St. Francis of Assisi, who was fond of saying, "What I am before God, that I am and nothing more," may have inspired Popeye's creator with this solid sense of reality.

It's a good frame of mind for approaching all situations where the job seems too big, but inescapable, like being asked to sell kisses at the bazaar, or to Be Perfect. Oh, well, you say, "I yam

---

[2] "Lift up your hearts."

what I yam. I'll do the *best* I can and let the chips fall where they may."

I have a variation on this. It's "Be a Cactus!" It owes something to the slogan St. Bernard gave his monks, "Be ye cisterns," but not much. St. Bernard told them to be cisterns because cisterns are deep, cool and quiet, unlike babbling brooks and leaky faucets, and they store water from which others may draw at any time without becoming depleted themselves. It's the apex of contemplative apostolicity. I simply haven't reached this stage.

"Be a Cactus" was my husband's idea, and I have a feeling it wasn't meant to be a compliment. "Look," he said, "go ahead and *get* the works of Tertullian if you want them, and don't worry about not liking to do the ironing plain. Some women may actually like to iron and want nothing else, but who cares if you don't? Stop trying to be a lily, or a shrinking violet, or a night-blooming cereus! If you happen to be a cactus, Be a Cactus!"

My husband isn't the voice of authority for nothing. He's written more of this book than he'll ever know. Nobody ever sizes me up so well, to my face. Frankly, though, after the first shock to my pride, I liked this slogan. The more I thought about it, the more "Be a Cactus" seemed to be just the one for me. I would try to be God's little cactus!

Just think a minute about the cactus. If you had never seen one or a picture of one and somebody described it to you, you might want to call him a liar. A cactus has to be seen to be believed. What's more, there are some thousand varieties, all native to the New World, all growing in incredible shapes ranging from "Organ-Pipe Cactus" to "Bishop's Hat" and "Purple Hedgehog." I forbore telling my husband the night-blooming cereus is a cactus, because I didn't know it then either. Like the Carmelites, it wakes up in the middle of the night to give glory to God. Being a cactus gives you a very wide field of play.

It's also tough. It normally stands out in the open, completely exposed, but protects itself quite well, thank you, by virtue of its bristles and spines. I have a sneaking suspicion it was this prickly aspect my husband had particularly in mind, but to continue: the cactus is a desert plant and needs practically nothing for its support. That's because its roots spread very, very far and it catches every little bit of food and moisture that's to be had. It manages to stay green where everything else dries up and blows away. Definitely, its leaf does not wither.

Most remarkable of all, it manages to produce outlandishly beautiful blossoms just where you'd expect them least: from the same places the bristles grow. Sometimes these blossoms turn into fruit, some of which makes pretty good preserves. As well as any cistern, the cactus manages to store water in its insides which has saved the life of many a parched traveler and is the ordinary refuge of all kinds of small animals and wildlife. Big cactuses provide about all the shade there is in open desert. Some are edible. Others can be dried and used for fuel and frames for houses.

Smaller ones can thrive in hothouses, or like the housewife, in almost any house, growing on windowsills even when nobody remembers to water them. I'll leave you to draw all the other obvious analogies.

Definitely, I promised, I'll try to BE A CACTUS!

I'm still trying, so I haven't made any headway yet toward a Latin motto. I do have my eye on a French one. It's *Toute la Corbeille!* and might be translated "Shoot the works!" I got it from St. Thérèse, who wasn't a little cactus, but a Little Flower. She didn't see any sense in shooting for Purgatory either.

In her *Autobiography*, as you may remember, she tells about the time her sister Leonie, who had just gotten too big to play with dolls, brought a whole basket (*corbeille*) filled with doll clothes, scraps for making more, and her doll as well, to pass on to her younger sisters.

"Here, my dears," she said. "Choose whatever you like." Therese's sister put in her hand and picked out a wad of braid that struck her fancy, but not Therese. She stopped to think a minute, then put out her hand and announced, "I choose everything!"

Then she proceeded to take the whole basket without further ado. Nobody objected because, after all, she had been asked to take anything she wanted and was well within her rights.

Writing many years later of this incident in the *Autobiography*, Thérèse drew the following conclusions from it:

I think this trait of my childhood characterizes the whole of my life; and when I began to think seriously of perfection I knew that to become a saint one had to suffer much, always aim at perfection and forget one's self. I saw that one could be a saint in varying degrees for we are free to respond to Our Lord's invitation by doing much or little in our love for Him; to choose, that is, between the sacrifices He asks. Then, just as before, I cried: "I choose everything!" My God, I do not want to be a saint by halves. I am not afraid to suffer for Your sake; I only fear doing my own will, so I give it to You and choose everything You will.

Me too. *Toute la Corbeille!* Pins and all.
What's your motto?

VI. THINGS

By now you must know I'm fond of Latin. The longer I live, the less I can see how a housewife gets along without it. For instance: without it she might very well miss the great truths unfolded monthly in the home magazines, tucked away as they are between those recipes for triple-tiered mauve and pink gelatin desserts for children's quick lunches and how to arrange petunias in a spittoon.

I remember one article in particular about how a fireplace, must be the focus of the living room. If you don't have a fireplace, said the author, you have to fake one, and told how, with pictures. You have to have a focus, and it should be a fireplace.

That's where the Latin comes in. If I hadn't studied Latin, how would I ever have known that the word *focus*, which is Latin, means fireplace, or hearth? The article was telling me to make the fireplace the fireplace, and sounder advice couldn't be given—or taken. I began by throwing the home magazine in and starting a cheery blaze, putting all the articles in focus (heh! heh!) at once.

This made me think of God, because it's impossible to look into a fire for any length of time without thinking about God, any more than you can look at dirt without thinking of sin. St. John of the Cross calls God the "Living Flame of Love," and never tires of drawing analogies of the soul burning with love of God to a log in a consuming fire. It would seem that God Himself suggested this identification of His divinity with flame. It was from a burning bush that God the Father declared Himself to Moses. The Sacred Heart of God the Son appears surrounded by flames and is invoked in the Litany as "burning furnace of charity." The Holy Spirit descended upon the infant Church at Pentecost in parted tongues of fire, and when we pray to the Holy Spirit, we ask to be "kindled in the fire of His love." Most delicate touch of all, Jesus in His humanity, as a parting gesture of great charm for us before the

Ascension, laid a homely little fire by the side of Lake Genesareth and fried fish on it for His Apostles' breakfast.

God is all light, all warmth. He is the Focus of all His creation. He must be the Focus of the home. Voltaire said that if there were no God man would have to invent Him, just like the magazine said to fake that fireplace! It's sound spiritual instinct that leads the Catholic homemaker to hang the big family Crucifix over the fireplace. This is interior decoration at its best. Art is symbol. To be real art, it must reflect truth. The crucifix, bearing the Figure that draws all things to Himself, has its sacramental type in the family hearth. All are drawn automatically to its light and heat, which in their turn are symbols of knowledge and love—God's knowledge, God's love.

From the most ancient times, men have gathered around a fire as they have gathered around an altar. The sturdy old Roman civilization, not in its decadence, but in its heyday as conqueror of Carthage and Moloch, was a civilization of families whose homes revolved around the hearth and the little household gods, the *lares* and *penates* known to every schoolchild with a Latin book. Centuries of paganism were able to pervert, but never to eradicate man's elemental orientation toward his Creator.

The Church, who sees in things the messages God put in them for us, has a special blessing for fire. It's one of her most ancient, and it reads: "O Lord God, almighty Father, unfailing Light! Who art the Source of all Light, do Thou sanctify this new fire, that after the darkness of this world, we may come with pure hearts to Thee, Who art perpetual Light."

The Church has blessings for herbs, typewriters, bees, bells, lard, wheelchairs, animals, chalk, so many things, because she understands the true significance of things and the part they play in leading us to God, or away from Him, depending on our approach to them. Hear St. Teresa:

> Everything that a God so great and so wise has created must have very many secrets from which we may learn, and those who know some of them do so. Still, I believe that there are more than anyone can understand in every little thing that God has made, even though it be but an ant.

Poets know this too. Tennyson put it this way:

Flower in the crannied wall,
I pluck you out of the crannies,
I hold you here, root and all, in my hand,
Little flower—but if I could understand
What you are, root and all, and all in all,
I should know what God and man is.

In His ineffable love, God Himself at the Incarnation entered personally into His material universe in order to sacramentalize His entire creation—to lead us not just by analogy, but sacramentally, from things seen to those unseen. The beautiful Christmas Preface sums up the purpose of the Incarnation in these terms and no other: "that through Him Whom we have come to know in visible form, we may be caught up [the Latin says "ravished"] into the love of the invisible."

No human being has ever lacked time to read. He may not have had time, or the skill, to read books, but books are only an infinitesimal part of what we should be reading. The housewife, for instance, can easily skip the last issue of *House Gorgeous* and simply read the house instead. There's a lot in it besides dirt.

Printed words are after all only symbols. They are little stylized signs that stand for something else—objects or concepts. Outside revelation and the prayer of the mystics, all human knowledge is derived by means of analogy. We manipulate symbols representing realities which are of themselves difficult to manipulate (like figuring mileage to the moon, or handing a neighbor a recipe for a cake instead of the cake itself).

These symbols may be words. They may be numbers. They may also be things. We live daily by means of signs. Some, like the number 3, have a universal, invariable meaning for most of us. Some signs have individual and highly variable meanings, like the antique clock face without hands across the desk from me now. I don't know what a handless clock says to you, but to me it says "eternity, timelessness." It rather settles my nerves on the busier days.

The house is the housewife's basic spiritual handbook. God puts her in her house and, through the things and the people in it, He instructs her. She especially is close to the matter of the

Sacraments and the parables: bread and leaven, salt, oil, water, the family table, fish, moths, rust. The lost coin the woman found in Scripture still disappears and reappears between the sofa cushions or in the floor cracks. Everything speaks—even the children's Saturday night bath, which is a homely type of the cleansing confession before the Sunday Eucharist.

Water is a beautiful symbol of grace throughout Scripture, but we are by no means limited to the figures found in the Bible. What about electricity, itself unseen, its effects so stupendous? Every incandescent light bulb is a symbol of a soul in the state of grace. Every dim, dying one is a symbol of a soul in habitual venial sin. The dead ones, alas, no electricity, no life of grace. And the bulbs which are good, but not turned on: the unbaptised!

God utters "Let there be light!" every time a switch is flicked. From stove to shaver, the modern house runs on electric power as the Church runs on the life of God, Who allows us to discover ever new marvels in the physical universe to teach us His truth as they minister to our needs. "For since the creation of the world His invisible attributes are clearly seen—His everlasting power also and divinity—being understood through the things that are made," says St. Paul *(Rom. 1:20).*

But it needn't be anything so cosmic as electricity. Take windowpanes. They illustrate easily how distractions in prayer work. Out our living room window is a mountain view stretching out like eternity. When I'm outdoors, I enjoy it freely. From indoors, my eye finds itself stopping first at everything closest to it, at the furniture, at the window mullions, finally at the specks on the panes, before it focuses on the view itself. If the smudges are too bad, I see the view only with difficulty, no matter how hard I try, though I know the view is there, that it's worth seeing, and that it's larger than anything between me and it.

In the same way a silly preoccupation with dinner can obstruct prayer. Dinner is nothing compared to God, yet enclosed as we are in our world of sense, dinner seems to have more substance. Momentarily, it obscures God as the spot on the window obscures the mountain. As long as we remain in this life we remain, as it were, indoors, within ourselves. Everything closest to our senses looms large. To see the view, we must learn to see past the furniture, keep looking out, and above all, keep the windows clean!

St. John of the Cross got a different story from windowpanes. One of his most famous passages on the spiritual life compares God's effect on the soul in contemplation to,

> ...the sun upon a window, infusing itself therein, and making it bright, so that all the stains and spots which formerly appeared upon it are lost from sight; but when the sun departs again the obscurities and stains appear upon it once more.

He was very fond of this figure and often compared the soul to a pane which resists God by its stains and imperfections as soiled and distorted glass impedes sunlight.

Our Lord put it even more simply: "If thy eye be sound, thy whole body will be full of light" *(Matt. 6:28)*.

In His public life Jesus taught almost entirely by analogies of this kind, drawn from the most commonplace things. Many of these figures reflect the hidden years at home where He had watched His mother at her housework, washing, mending and cooking.

"If the salt loses its strength, what shall it be salted with?" He asked His disciples *(Matt. 5:13)*.

"And no one puts a patch of raw cloth on an old garment, for the patch tears away from the garment, and a worse rent is made. Nor do people pour new wine into old wineskins, else the skins burst, the wine is spilt, and the skins are ruined" *(Matt. 9:17)*.

"The kingdom of heaven is like leaven, which a woman buried in three measures of flour, until all of it was leavened" *(Matt. 13:3)*.

"Clean first the inside of the cup and of the dish, that the outside too may be clean" *(Matt. 23:26)*.

There is no end to what things teach us. If I were to pursue the subject, I would have to say like St. John that "not even the world itself, I think, could hold the books that would have to be written" *(John 21:25)*.

Things, however, reveal God's order only when they are used properly. Their symbolism is inextricably bound up with their function. A windowpane used as anything but a windowpane could tell St. John of the Cross nothing. For a housewife, the house speaks in just the proportion that she administers it rightly.

Things can be treacherous. Not privileged to take a vow of poverty, a housewife either falls into avarice, collecting more and more of them wildly as a cancer does cells, till the house bulges; or else she ends by neglecting them and despising them utterly as just more stuff to dust. I suppose only saints can really steer the middle course between these two vices and respect a thing as it should be respected, as a *thing*.

A housewife's rule over the things of her house is her rule over that part of material creation entrusted to her and for which she will have to render account. In a high sense, her rule over her house reflects her rule over herself. There is more than a symbolic relationship between the cleanliness of her windowpanes and the state of her soul. She doesn't have the right to break a cup carelessly any more than she has the right to lose her temper carelessly, or willfully to impair her health.

Things in themselves are good, and it is the particular vocation of the laity to use them in a good manner, for good ends. Cups and saucers, rugs and tables are not to be used irresponsibly or contemptuously, "because creation itself also will be delivered from its slavery to corruption unto the freedom of the glory of the sons of God" *(Rom. 8:21)*.

We were never created to fly around in a vacuum. At the end of time, a glorification of material nature will take place that staggers our imagination. Don't take my word for it. Here is what a famous theologian, M.J. Scheeben, says in his *Mysteries of Christianity*:

> Not only the human body, but the whole of material nature, is moving toward a state of glorification, in which it is to realize its final purpose and attain its eternal repose.
> We have to view this transformation according to the analogy of the glorification of the human body, with which it is closely connected. For as the body is the domicile of the soul, material nature is the domicile of the whole man. The human body is derived from material nature and does not abandon its organic connection with matter even when united to the spirit. By a natural conformity, therefore, the glorification of the human body must be communicated to the nature which encompasses it and is bound up with it, so that this nature may become a worthy dwelling place for glorified

man, and in its totality have a share in the glory shed over man, its highest pinnacle. ... This glorification is for material nature as much a complete transformation and rebirth to a higher existence and life, a new heavenly creation, as is the sanctification and transfiguration of the soul by grace.

I guess those windowpanes could be cleaner.

VII. SAINTE SOLANGE

Back in the days when I thought housework was beneath me, instead of way above me as I now know it is, I used to do freelance feature writing. Every now and then I'd get a by-line, and my name would appear on top of what I wrote.

Came the day when a little old lady with white hair, used to speaking her mind, asked me point blank, "How in the world did you ever think up a crazy pen name like that? How do you pronounce it?"

"Solahnge," I said. And I thought it only right to add that I hadn't made it up. Solange happens to be my name, and if, as they say, *nomen est omen*, I couldn't be more pleased with it, if I had thought it up myself.

"What's in a name?" A lot. Juliet brushed aside the fact that Romeo was a Montague with "a rose by any other name would smell as sweet." Well, if she meant a thing is what it is, all right; but if she meant to imply that what a thing is called is purely arbitrary and accidental, I can only say her sense of reality didn't go very deep. She was young and callow, and with that attitude, it's small wonder she died a suicide. If she thought a rose is called a rose by accident, or that Romeo was called Montague by accident, she betrayed herself right there as the materialist she really was, though she was called a Catholic.

It's no use pretending words don't fascinate me, for the preceding pages prove they do. Like sex, they're full of mystery. They're so full of mystery they can easily become a kind of heresy all on their own. This heresy is *cabala*, and people who mistake words for what words represent fall into it. It's a sort of magic, and happily, it isn't much in fashion today. Unhappily, the opposite vice, which may have been Romeo's, is very much in fashion, and symptomatic of sacramental anemia.

Whoever trifles with names trifles with immanent being. Holy Writ is full of reverence for names, from the never to be

34

pronounced Yahweh right down to the name given to the littlest bug by Adam at God's command. There is nothing accidental about the names in Scripture, because to the Hebrews a name is a word which veils an inner reality, thereby revealing it.

When a name ceases to express reality, its life is gone, and it has become meaningless. Speech full of meaningless words and names is the speech of a civilization devoid of religion. The fireplace, let's say, is no longer the *focus*. It's just a fireplace, and can be put anywhere.

In Scripture, and in all great mythologies, whenever a child is born who is destined to be somebody, the meaning of his name is either obvious, or more often than not, carefully explained. By the same token, when God converts a human being in maturity, so that his inner being suffers an entire transformation, this metamorphosis is almost always expressed socially by a change in name. Obviously this must be so, because the creature is no longer the same.

Abram the pagan becomes Abraham after the Promise. After wrestling the angel, Jacob becomes Israel, "who strove with God." Simon the fisherman becomes Cephas the Rock. Saul, the Pharisee, becomes Paul, the Apostle to the Gentiles. Still today, a layman entering religious life is often given a new name when he dons his habit.

So calling a spade a spade, if it is a spade, is even more important than might at first appear. Let Juliet call a rose by another name if she pleases. She was young and full of vapors.

God the Father, Who endlessly begets His Son, utters the WORD. This is the closest revelation can bring our understanding to an ineffable procession of pure spirit. Every human word, or name, is a reflection of this action which takes place in the bosom of the Most Holy Trinity. When a human being clothes with speech an intellectual concept which he generates spiritually, he performs a figurative action of transcendent import. The WORD, Scripture tells us, became flesh. Human words, where spirit and matter cooperate to express an idea in time, are figures of the Incarnate God. Speakers speak with these, and writers write with these. To a thinking human being, the responsibility is terrible, because he is always at grips with truth.

Words are therefore to be treated with respect, as any other channels of grace. This same Incarnate God turned to His Father in heaven and taught us to say, "Hallowed be Thy *Name*," because what God is called is the glory of what God is. He is Yahweh, I AM, a name which can be applied to nothing else existing.

His Son, the WORD, was clothed with a human name at His Circumcision. "His name was called Jesus, the name given Him by the angel before He was conceived in the womb" *(Luke 2:21)*. Jesus means Saviour, because that is what He is.

This Jesus came to tell us, "Whatever you ask in my *name*, that I will do" *(John 14:13)*, because to ask in His *name*, means in a sense to *be* Him, to ask as He would ask. He gave us His own name when He became incarnate with us.

To know who a person is, his real name must be known, the one God creates for him individually when He sanctifies him. The vast majority of us don't know our names yet. All we know is that there is one just for us, and no duplicates. St. John heard the angel in the vision say, "To him who overcomes, I will give the hidden manna, and I will give him a white pebble, and upon the pebble a new name written, which no one knows except him who receives it" *(Apoc. 2:17)*.

Now, my patroness is called Solange, and I could never have made her up. Almighty God did. She doesn't need my defense, but I could no more leave her out of this book than I could appear on television without saying hello to the family back home in front of the set. Solange is really somebody, and ever since the little old lady's question, I've been looking for the chance to say so.

I'll have to come clean on one point, however. Solange isn't a housewife, and never was. She was a French shepherdess and a virgin martyr, but vulgar. She's so vulgar she comes under the general heading of "popular saints," which means everybody recognized her sanctity without being told, the Church approving her cult much later. She has never been raised to the altars of the universal Church, her official veneration being of obligation only in the Diocese of Bourges, but this is nothing against her. Lots of saints start this way.

While Charlemagne's grandsons divided up the Holy Roman Empire, Solange quietly tended her sheep in the fields of

Villemont, a tiny hamlet in the old province of Berry, along the banks of the Ouatier. Popular art shows her twirling her distaff, as shepherdesses are supposed to do while the sheep munch. Sometimes there's a book on her lap, but considering her times and her station, it's not likely she was able to read it. Her crook lies to hand, and a faithful dog is on the lookout. The sky is blue, and chock full of angels. I don't think the political unrest of her day distressed her much, because she spent most of her time alone with God and the sheep. Besides, she was pretty, and that led to troubles of her own.

Some 800 years after her death, a provincial historian whose own name is Gaspard Thaumas de la Thaumassière, distilled a few facts about Ste. Solange in his *Histoire du Berry*, published in 1689. Not much bothered by grammar, he tells us:

> Ste. Solange lived at the time of Frotaire, Archbishop of Bourges (876-890), in the village of Villemont, Parish of St. Martin-du-Crot, now called Parish of Ste. Solange, three leagues distant from the city of Bourges.
>
> Being endowed with singular beauty, its report spread throughout all the province and reached the ears of the local prince's son, who was Bernard, Count of Poitiers and of Bourges.
>
> At the account of Solange's beauty, he became curious to see her, pretended to go hunting in the direction of her parish, and running into her in a field where she was tending her sheep, he was instantly smitten with her to the depths of his soul.
>
> He dismounted, tried to convince her of his love and the resolution he had taken to make her Lady and Countess of the district by making her his wife.
>
> This chaste and wise shepherdess told him that from childhood she had chosen Jesus Christ as spouse and to Him she had consecrated her virginity, which she wished to preserve inviolate.
>
> He insists, and driven by carnal love, tries to do her violence; she tries to escape by flight. He pursues her on horseback. He picks her up and puts her on the saddle before him. Having vainly tried entreaty, threats and force to persuade her to condescend to his unhappy design, she throws herself to the ground, thereby so enraging the young lord, whom her refusal had made furious, that he drew his sword and cut off her head, which though separated from her body, pronounced three times the name of her chaste and divine Spouse, Jesus.
>
> And taking up her head in her hands, she carried it to the church of St. Martin where she herself chose her burial place.

It's a violent tale concerning a most gentle creature and bears certain marked resemblances to that of the Welsh Saint Winifred, who suffered the same fate for the same reason about 200 years before. There is nothing implausible about the crime. In our own days St. Maria Goretti continues the long tradition of martyrs to virginity, who seem to arise especially in times which have little practical use for that state.

Nor is there any reason to believe that the nobleman's offer of marriage is necessarily a pious euphemism. Bernard's character stands out very neatly through Thaumas' few lines: a spoiled brat used to getting anything he wanted. He may have actually been handsome. He was certainly even more proud than profligate, and highly conscious of his social position.

Had he intended mere rape, he would hardly have bothered to chop off his victim's head. He evidently was so taken with her that he not only descended to making love to her, but actually did offer her marriage and a title. Whether he meant it or not doesn't change the story. Anything to get his way. One tradition states he was a second son, and this opens up a whole psychological vista. Perhaps in the wake of a sober older brother slated to inherit the ducal crown, Bernard had been allowed considerable freedom from responsibility.

But propose to Solange he must have. What utterly enraged him was that after this unheard of condescension on his part, the girl had the effrontery to refuse him. Him! Aside from his personal charms, he was Count of Poitiers, son of the powerful Due de Berry. And she was a peasant. A peasant who herded sheep!

As for the reason she gave him for her refusal, that was the last straw and a plain lie. Bernard, like a great many people in our own day, simply couldn't imagine anyone outside the cloister loving God that much. Anybody knows a girl who really feels like that becomes a nun and gets out of sane people's way. And certainly no *pretty* girl ever feels like that! Virginity in the world, God knows, has never had an easy time of it.

Bernard, who wouldn't want to play second fiddle to God in any case, burned with humiliation, for to the self-centered, all affronts are personal. Beside himself with rage, he chased her on horseback, not just because that was faster, but no doubt because this afforded him protection from Solange's dog, who must have been thoroughly alerted by now. If she were built like most Berrichon peasant girls, Solange must have put up a desperate fight, but we know Bernard ended by killing her in a fit of blind passion. It was just another instance in which lust is credited with a crime which only anger and pride could execute.

What the noble Bernard's fate was I don't know. In the ninth century, his exalted birth would most probably have kept him well above the law, certainly where a barefoot girl was concerned. There is a strong local tradition, however, that his conscience-stricken family built at Bourges the ancient church of St. Pierre-le-Puellier, no longer extant, in an honest attempt to repair as best they could his unwarranted outrage to Almighty God. Let's hope that whoever was charged with his upbringing did extra penance.

The little saint herself, who like all saints didn't mind losing her head over virtue, became almost immediately an object of popular devotion. Pilgrims flocked to her tomb, multiplying reports of her sanctity and marvels, and the little parish of St. Martin became that of Ste. Solange. She must not have been unknown to a later French shepherdess called Jeanne d'Arc, who lived near the aforesaid church of St. Pierre while she stayed in Bourges managing the king's troops. Tending sheep, it would seem, can prepare one for anything! Though not so famous as Jeanne, Solange has long been the patron of her province and has forged beyond, even having a suburban church in Paris to her honor, and a mosaic at Lourdes.

Although her life hovers on the legendary, our friend Thaumas wasn't a historian without scruples. His account of her neglects to mention, for instance, a certain bright star which is supposed to have been seen over Solange's head as she walked along the banks of the stream making her meditations. Furthermore, his salient facts are amply corroborated in the Saint's earliest liturgy, as well as in the diocesan history of the Archbishops of Bourges. (The latter was long preserved in the Augustinian convent and drawn upon heavily by Father Honoré Niquet, Rector of the Jesuit College, who wrote a definitive life of the Saint in 1653 on which the Bollandists in turn drew.)

Now I like plain unadorned facts as well as anybody, but I don't mind a little embroidery if it means something. There's no point in throwing out the baby with the bath water. I like that star. Whether it can be seen by the public or not, every saint lives under a star, because ever since the Magi, a star hovers where Christ is. St. Dominic has been allowed to keep his, and personally, I have no objection to Solange's just because there's no ironclad proof of it. Like the Blessed Virgin, Solange was a lay contemplative, the most hidden kind of saint there is. A visible star must have been a great help to anyone privileged to *find* her. I'm happy to say the liturgical commission which revised her office in 1917 agreed with me. Acting under the influence of St. Pius X's *Divino Afflatu*, they put the star back into the lessons of the second Nocturn.

There's something else I like about Solange, and there's no proof for that either: she's a *sainte céphalophore*. That means she carried her head in her hands. French saints, perhaps because they spring from an intellectual nation, seem to have a weakness for carrying their severed heads around. St. Denis, Bishop of Paris, beheaded for the faith in Roman times, is probably the most famous of these, though the fashion in France seems to have been started in Apostolic times by St. Valeria, beheaded in Limoges. Naturally, you don't have to believe this marvel, but I think you do have to believe what it symbolizes in folk hagiography, because what it symbolizes is true.

Where Solange is concerned, I think it's the key to her whole personality. If she didn't pick up her head and carry it to her parish church, she should have, and all the vulgar people around Bourges thought so, which is why the story has come down to us. She had to carry her head, because her name is *Solange*.

There have been several fanciful explanations of this name. Renaissance preachers liked to trace its derivation from *Solis Angelus*—angel of the sun—no doubt dwelling at length on that star floating over her head. More rational research admits Solange was probably originally a place, Soulange or Soulonge, which in turn was a corruption of the Latin name *Solonius*, the ancient owner of a nearby Roman villa in the days when France was Gallia.

Good sense inclines one to the latter explanation, just as it would be silly to deny that Juliet's rose is derived from anything but the Greek *rhodon*, but that tells us precious little about the rose Juliet had in mind. And Solonius tells us nothing about Solange.

Her name begins where? When? In the mind of God, I suppose, as all things must. When we first pick it up, it belongs to a man, then to a place, then to Solange and another place, always undergoing that constant and subtle metamorphosis by which the life principle in language is perceived.

For language is a creature of God and reveals Him as all creatures must, according to its nature. It moves like a gentle torrent flowing over a countryside, penetrating and caressing everything in its way. Man has no more been able to create a language than he has been able to create a duck.

If you belong to my generation, maybe you once studied Esperanto. It's one of some 200 made up "international" languages supposed to solve once and for all the world's Babel problem. It's a real Frankenstein monster, and like the monster, it's contrived of bits and scraps of live, God-created tissue taken from all the European tongues, with prefixes, suffixes and infixes, and a most remarkable lack of grammar or irregularity. Again like the monster, it has absolutely no soul, and despite all kinds of artificial respiration, it can't be made to live like life. Its word for chatter, incidentally, is *babil*. "Ĝi ne intenc'as anstatau'i la naci'a' j'n lingv'o'j'n." My old American Esperanto Key translates this as: "It not intends to replace the national languages." There's no danger of that. It couldn't. The Key also says, "Proper names should be written in their own languages." Well, that's a mercy. That means Solange will easily survive Esperanto and continue to move and become according to God's mysterious will, as she did on earth.

That being the case, we can indulge in a little vulgar fantasy, such as common people like. Solange is a very vulgar name. As it stands today, it finds itself composed of two equally vulgar, quite ordinary French words: *sol* and *ange*. *Sol* is ground, or soil, what the Hebrews called *adamah*, the same old stuff Adam was named after and to which we all return. Ange is, of course, an angel. So Solange is an earth-angel. That means she's matter and spirit, like all of us. She is a sacrament, as all saints are sacraments. She is a word, reflecting the Word, like all of us.

Being body and soul, earthly and angelic, it's quite proper for her to carry her head in her hands, because as she thinks, she does. Her spiritual powers are perfectly borne by her physical powers. She symbolizes not just action, not just contemplation, but the full perfection of the mixed life. She carried her head to her parish church because that's where it belonged.

"My soul is ever in my hands," cried King David *(Ps. 118:109)*, who knows what I'm trying to say.

The Collect from Solange's Mass has caught the idea perfectly. It reads:

> Lord Jesus Christ, who have established your dwelling in the chaste heart of Blessed Solange, your Virgin and Martyr, grant that we may imitate *in the integrity of her faith and her life*, her whose merits we celebrate by our pious homage.

Anne Boleyn's ghost is said to carry its head in its hands, too. ("Tucked underneath her arm," I believe the old song has it.) And small wonder, for as all of us think, we do, sinners as well as saints. Poor Anne! Losing her head was just as much a natural consequence of her thinking as was Solange's, but what a difference!

After Solange's head was severed from her body, her mouth uttered three words: *Jésus! Jésus! Jésus!* This needn't surprise us, for they are the Word which every saint utters as he breathes, living or dying.

> Truncato licet capite
> Ter Jesum inclamat voce
> Caput manu portans pie,

sings her eighteenth century liturgy.

Popular legend understands a thing or two! It exasperates rationalists and delights "little ones." Everybody knew Ste. Solange would have said that from her severed head, if she could have said anything. Whether she actually did or not, let historians haggle over, or the people who teach "the Bible as history" in broadminded universities. Solange's friends understand perfectly.

She herself continues to speak Christ and still carries her head in her hands under that marvelous star. She is quite naturally invoked as a protector of youthful purity, and she's a thaumaturge, but all her miracles have a distinctly earthly flavor. Even in heaven she doesn't mind concentrating on the temporal needs of her suppliants.

The hymn for Vespers on her feast runs,

> Redditur caeco sua lux, et auris
> Redditur surdo, sua lingua muto,
> Impari qui oix pede claudus ibat
> Ambulat aequo,

telling of her gift of sight to the blind, hearing to the deaf, speech to the mute, and an even walk to the limping, extending the work of her divine Master.

She's particularly known as a rain-maker and has saved her countryside from drought on innumerable occasions. Farmers, she remembers, like good crops, and when she brings the rains, it pours. She has quite a sense of humor, too. On her annual Whitmonday processions, she is said to bless particularly the fields that get trampled the hardest. A farmer who once refused to let the marchers across his hemp field got only a light sprinkle and lost his whole harvest, while everybody else's flourished.

In 1635 she rained out a Calvinist, just for fun. "Do you think cataracts from heaven are going to open up just because you walk her all over town?" The Calvinist spoofed, as her relics were borne by. It started pouring so hard he had to dash into his house before the words were out of his mouth. The old account doesn't say whether he was converted. Probably not.

She weathered the French Revolution quite well, thank you. When the Cistercians of Loroy were disbanded, such relics of her as they possessed were hidden in a belfry for the duration. Her other major relics were plundered from her parish church by *sans-culottes* who were primarily interested in the chased silver reliquary. Luckily the pious mayor, a certain Dr. Pellé, pretended to take part in the looting and actually managed to slip away with her bones, which the desecrators tossed aside as valueless. They were hidden in an outlying mill while *Liberté, Fraternité* and *Egalité* roamed madly over the land.

Far from running out on her province, however, Ste. Solange more than stood her ground. Incredible as it may seem, she got herself installed as titular patron of the new Masonic Lodge set up in Bourges. One of the Lodge's letterheads, preserved in the museum there, reads, *Loge de Ste. Solange,* and shows a pelican extending his wings over two S's. Lodge meetings, it seems, were held belowstairs in the former convent of St. Clare, while priests and sisters of Charity were imprisoned in the cells above.

Regardless of their hatred of the Church, the Lodge members evidently had nothing personal against Ste. Solange, who had always been their friend. She was *du pays,* anyway, sprung from their soil, and had lived her life with her bare feet in it. Although she was a virgin martyr, she could never be accused of ever having worn a religious habit, and that was what mattered to them. Besides, with all those aristocrats losing their heads to the guillotine, it was nice, I guess, to have a real decapitated peasant, decapitated by an aristocrat, on the other side to maintain balance.

As far as I know, Solange is the only saint in the calendar ever to pull off a *coup* like that. I nominate her patroness—not of Freemasonry, God forbid—but of freemasons, which is quite a different thing. She obviously had her eye on them in their beginnings, and being a shepherdess, she must have a special weakness for any kind of lost sheep.

Being now one of those who follow the Lamb wherever He goes, I guess Solange called by any other name would smell as sweet, but she wouldn't be Solange. At least, not to me, for

> An angel in the air
> Is here as well as there,
> But an angel on the ground
> Is right where she is found.
> Solange! Solange! Solange!

VIII. HOME RULE

"Tina ate my bacon!" wailed Stephen, looking from his plate to his little sister, who was licking her fingers contentedly.

"Serves you right for not getting here when you were called," I pontificated.

"I had to make my bed. Tavy slept on top of his covers last night so he wouldn't have to make his. That's why he's on time!"

"Tavy! Eat your egg. The white part, too." "Daddy didn't eat his."

Glare, glare.

"I don't like the white," Tavy ventured.

"You don't have to like it. You just have to eat it," singsonged Lydia, taking my favorite cliché right out of my mouth. She has reason to know it, having the most finicky appetite of the bunch.

"Listen to who's talking," noted my husband.

That's the trouble with living with other people. You can't get away with a darned thing. This sort of, well, constructive criticism is carried on during Chapter of Faults in religious communities, I'm told. Chapter is held now and then at set times, and proceeds according to set rules. At our house it goes on around the clock, seven days a week. It makes up in ruthless effectiveness for what it may lack in decorum. If it doesn't make you good, it makes you awfully careful.

Tina is our fifth child, which means she had six of us to learn from, right off the bat. Her first words were not "Ma-Ma" or "Da-Da," but those she heard the most: "Quit it!"

It astonishes me less and less how often holy religious look up to family life as a particularly crucifying path to God. Personally, I never understood family life at all until I studied the Rule of St. Benedict. Having said that, I can hear: "Oh, come now, you don't run a home like a monastery. I don't care how religious you are!" By "religious" most people who make this comment mean "crazy," but are too polite to say so.

But they're right, of course. You don't. That's putting the cart before the horse. The staggering truth is that you run a monastery like a home. St. Benedict certainly did.

When he entered history about 1400 years ago, hermits and wanderers were the rule rather than the exception among those seeking perfection. Benedict spent some years in the desert himself and had ample personal experience of the dangers of solitary life, devoid as it is of the checks and balances—and torture—of living with others. He was against living alone. You can do that safely, he said, only after a rigorous probation of living in one place with others. Otherwise, you're sure to fall into selfishness, pride and all the worst vices, barring an exceptional vocation from God.

St. Benedict was a great admirer of St. Basil, the patriarch of eastern monasticism who had come to the same conclusion some 150 years before. The common life is definitely preferable, says St. Basil:

> For him who falls into sin, the recovery of the right path is so much easier, for he is ashamed at the blame expressed by so many in common. ... There are still other dangers which we say accompany the solitary life; the first and greatest is that of self-satisfaction. For he who has no one to test his work easily believes that he has completely fulfilled the commandments. ...
>
> For how shall he manifest his humility, when he has no one to whom he can show himself the inferior? How shall he manifest compassion, cut off from the society of the many? How will he exercise himself in patience, if no one opposes his wishes?

How indeed?

Granted that living alone is bad for imperfect souls, still a certain seclusion is necessary in order to draw near to God, "to smooth the waxen tablet before attempting to write on it," as St. Basil put it. The problem is therefore: How to be alone with people around you?

"Get invited to a lot of big cocktail parties!" might be one answer. But that's worse than the desert.

St. Benedict's solution was much more obvious, and very holy. He patterned his new community, as St. Basil had, after the family, the natural social unit designed by God to nurture and draw souls to Him. He called his Rule "a little rule for beginners," and it was based on the littler rule just seen in operation at our breakfast table, but raised to a higher power.

The monks who live a family life are "the strongest kind of monks," said St. Benedict, and they are called cenobites, from the Greek κόινος, common, and βίος, life. That means they lead a life in common, polishing each other's sharp edges off by rubbing elbows in the monastery, as opposed to hermits and anchorites, who go it alone.

I'm not a monk, but I'm a cenobite. So are the children. My husband's a cenobite too, and in many ways he has it even worse than we do, because he's in charge.

It's no accident that the head of a monastery is called an Abbot, a word derived from *abba*, the Hebrew word for father, nor that all the monks take a vow of obedience to him, to obey him as children do their natural father.

"The third degree of humility," says St. Benedict's Rule, "is that a man for the love of God subject himself to his superior in all obedience." Well, it's humiliating to admit we haven't got even the first degree around here. There must be some humility in that.

The father of the family, like the Abbot, stands in the place of God, "from Whom is all fatherhood." The family conforms to God's will by obeying the father's will, for obedience is a sustaining sacramental lifeline second only to the Holy Eucharist. We may receive Communion only once a day, but we can obey around the clock.

Obedience is considered so important among cenobites, each monk makes it a special vow—just like the housewife who marries a husband. It sacramentalizes even the most inconsequential action because under obedience, immediate and intimate contact is established with God's authority. It's almost as if He performed the action Himself. A wife and children who can't see God's will in the husband and father's and cannot obey for supernatural reasons, submitting their judgment when they disagree, are dissolving the spiritual cement of their home. Monks who can't do this are told to leave.

This puts father permanently on the spot. What St. Benedict says about the Abbot applies in every way to him:

The Abbot should always remember what he is and what he is called, and should know that to whom more is committed, from him more is required. Let him also understand how difficult and arduous a task he has undertaken, of ruling souls and adapting himself to many dispositions. One he must humor, another rebuke, another persuade, according to each one's disposition and understanding, and thus adapt and accommodate himself to all in such a way, that he may not only suffer no loss in the flock committed to him, but may even rejoice in the increase of a good flock.

It's important for the polishing process that cenobites not be of their own choosing. Brothers and sisters in a family choose to live with each other even less than do monks in a monastery, but live together they must! This is probably hardest of all on the Abbot. St. Benedict says,

> ... above all let him not have greater solicitude for fleeting, earthly, and perishable things, and so overlook or undervalue the salvation of the soul committed to him; but let him always remember that he has undertaken the government of souls and will have to give an account of them. And if he be tempted to complain of lack of means, let him remember the words: *Seek ye first the kingdom of God and his approval, and all these things shall be yours without asking.* ... and while by his admonitions he is helping others to amend, he himself is cleansed of his faults.

The Prior is supposed to help him out. This is the monastic office which in point of authority most represents the wife's, and St. Benedict had it pegged as a trouble spot right from the beginning. He had a good bit to say about priors who are,

> ... puffed up by an evil spirit of pride, who regard themselves as equal to the abbot, and arrogating to themselves tyrannical power foster troubles and dissensions in the community.... Hence arise envies, quarrels, detractions, rivalries, dissensions, and disorders. For, while the abbot and prior are at variance, it must needs be that their souls are endangered by this dissension.

Was there ever a better description of a home where Mom wanted to wear the pants?

St. Benedict countenances only a Prior who,

> ... [shall] respectfully perform what is enjoined him by his abbot, and do nothing contrary to the abbot's will or regulations; for the more he is set

above the rest, the more scrupulously should he observe the precepts of the Rule.

The Saint goes on to say that incorrigible priors must be deposed from office or even expelled from the monastery. Well, of course, in married life, it isn't that easy to get rid of the Prior. The Abbot here is certainly stuck with his.

Parallels between a home and a monastery are endless because they aren't parallels. Every monastery is simply a very Christian home where the routine of living is made to serve a life of prayer. Chores are divided up according to age and ability. The common good is considered in all decisions; property belongs to none and all, with distribution made according to need.

The family sleeps and eats together under one roof. They read. They pray together. They garden and wash clothes. Guests are received as they should be received in every home, "like Christ, for He will say, 'I was a stranger and you took me in'" *(Rule of St. Benedict, Ch. 53)*.

The home is the natural setting, furthermore, for the Christian practice of corporal and spiritual works of mercy. It's in the home first of all that the hungry are fed, the naked clad and sinners admonished and prayed for. Because the sinner happens to be one's own ten-year-old and right there handy doesn't in any way diminish the value of the act. If he comes down with chickenpox, reading him a story in bed qualifies as "visiting the sick" just as much as if he were some stranger in the county hospital.

There is one monk in particular whose duties are very much like the housewife's. (I notice it takes quite a few people to fill all the housewife's roles.) He's called the Cellarer, and the Rule states he should be "prudent, of mature character, temperate, not a great eater, not proud, not headstrong, not rough-spoken, not lazy, not wasteful," in other words, just about perfect. If every man chose his wife with the care with which St. Benedict chose his Cellarer, standards would certainly go up, and I might never have got married.

Listen to this:

> Let him have charge of everything. ... Let him look upon all the utensils of the monastery and its whole property as upon the sacred vessels of the altar.

St. Benedict had no illusions about the true value of *things!* He continues:

> Let him not think that anything may be neglected. Let him neither practice avarice nor be wasteful and a squanderer of the monastery's substance, but let him do all things with measure. ... Above all things let him have humility!

Here's something to meditate on when dinner is cold sandwiches—and late—for reasons unnamed:

> Let him give the brethren their appointed allowance of food without any arrogance or delay, that they not be scandalized, mindful of what the Scripture saith that he deserves "who shall scandalize one of these little ones" *(Matt. 18:6).*
>
> Let him take the greatest care of the sick, of children, of guests and of the poor, knowing without doubt that he will have to render an account for all of these on the Day of Judgment. ...
>
> Let those things which have to be asked for and those things that have to be given, be asked for and given at the proper times; so that no one may be troubled or vexed in the house of God.

A "house of God" doesn't have to be a monastery. A house of God is any house where God dwells. As St. Benedict clearly saw, any home contains in its very structure certain factors predisposing to sanctity if they're made use of. He simply selected and distilled these, raising them to a higher level. Even in their raw, natural state, these elements sanctify every family according to its degree of spiritual vitality.

In the Blessing for a House during Epiphany, the Roman Ritual makes this fact plain:

> Bless, O Lord, almighty God, this home, that it be the shelter of health, chastity, self-conquest, humility, goodness, mildness, obedience to the commandments and thanksgiving to God the Father, Son and Holy Spirit. May blessing remain for all time upon this dwelling and them that live herein.

All God's cenobites got high aims!
We can't miss, if we can just hold out.

IX. PARLOR, BEDROOM, AND THINK

"Look," I tell my Liddy over the kitchen sink, "I could never do dishes the way I do if I hadn't studied Greek."

She's skeptical.

"πάντα ρει" I shout, as the last of the suds disappear down the drain. "Everything flows," just as Heraclitus said. He probably never did a dish in his life, but he would understand what I mean, all right, being a philosopher. Nothing so gives tone to a pile of greasy plates as a fine classical quotation.

Lydia, who no doubt suspects I've forgotten more Greek than I ever knew, doesn't see the point at all. "Would algebra help?"

"Certainly. Of course, it would take somebody like St. Thomas Aquinas to do these dishes really right, you know."

Slight pause in which to visualize the Great "Dumb Ox" over our sink, with his wide sleeves rolled back from his patrician hands, harnessing his big heart and giant intellect to the operation.

Actually, this picture isn't too farfetched. As a Dominican novice he may have done dishes many a time. Heaven knows how much of the *Summa* may have lain hidden in soapsuds.

By the way, have you ever *really* looked at soapsuds? Well, I won't take time for that now. The point is, it takes intelligence and love to perform manual tasks as rational and loving beings are meant to perform them.

"Look at St. Isaac Jogues. Think of all the university degrees he had, just to be sent out to spend his days among illiterate Hurons—and get his fingers chewed down by an Iroquois chief who couldn't spell cat!" I have a great devotion to St. Isaac (a name which means Laughter), and I nominate him unreservedly as the patron of egghead housewives, who normally do their best thinking surrounded by wild Indians.

"Do you think his education was accidental? That it didn't qualify his martyrdom in any way? That it didn't affect his prayer?" I hammered on.

"You mean a Ph.D.'s fingers taste better?"

That's really, I guess, what it amounts to, before God. Essentially, all other things being equal (which they never are), a Ph.D. getting his fingers chewed for love of God is a greater work than if he had been content with a B.A. As I said, I could never do dishes the way I do if I hadn't studied Greek. If I could remember more of it, I'd do them a lot better. Subjectively, too, it takes a heap of study to see the real point of doing dishes, or getting your fingers chewed.

St. Benedict would certainly bear me out. Outside choir, he provided only two occupations for his monks: manual labor and study. He had to provide two, because monks, like housewives and St. Isaac Jogues, are composed of body and soul. These have their separate interests and must be properly engaged. St. Benedict understood perfectly well that people often doodle when they concentrate hard, pray best when they kneel, and that all mathematics hinge on man's being able to count on his fingers and toes. The body works, supplying its physical needs and those of others. The soul thinks and wills. Both pray.

St. Benedict set his monks to cobbling, farm work, scrubbing, and cooking so they could study Scripture and theology realistically and pray fervently. Believe me, nothing so liberates the intellect as peeling potatoes. And conversely, nothing unlocks the secrets of the potato like meditating on the Psalms. These things go together like yin and yang, like Martha and Mary, like peanut butter and jelly.

In our rule of life, we cenobites have got it *made*, when it comes to manual labor. I trust I don't have to labor the point. I remember reading once about a hermit in the Egyptian desert who spent his time weaving and un-weaving large piles of rush mats to keep his body occupied between meals of "pulse" and stale water. No housewife need ever be reduced to mat un-weaving. There's plenty of work in every home, and none of it ever stays done.

She can have all the pulse she can cook, too. Pulse is any old cooked greens. Could be Popeye's spinach. I just found this out, and I'm passing the information along. It had worried me for years, thinking that was one ingredient of sanctity I'd have to go to Egypt for. With or without pulse, however, any woman who tries to sneak out of working with her hands when she has the opportunity just likes to do things the hard way. It's like trying to sneak out of humanity. Work is penance, as we have noted, but not intrinsically. The penance part of it has existed only since the Fall, like the rougher parts of marriage.

Both work and marriage existed "from the beginning," and were meant exclusively to be a source of joy and satisfaction to mankind, as reflections of God's creative power. I'm not making this up. Genesis tells us that God blessed Adam and Eve and told them to "fill the earth and subdue it." Before Eve was even created, "the Lord God took the man and placed him in the Garden of Eden to till it and to keep it," so there was no question of punishment in working.

Physical labor was ordained to fill a basic need of human nature, intrinsic to our being. It supplies a satisfaction we are starved without. Absence of physical activity creates a grave imbalance in the individual, as any doctor can verify, not only in the body, but in the psyche. Golf courses and gyms are filled with people whose daily lives deprive them of this legitimate satisfaction.

Why does scrubbing a floor stabilize thought processes? I don't know, but it does, particularly in women. Women who never work with their hands are proverbially "flighty." Occupational therapy—a fancy name for treating insane minds by keeping their bodies busy—is the oldest and still the most reliable cure known. Ideally, manual work is the pedestal upon which mental activity rests secure. It is the proper activity of the body, purposeful and real. Far from hindering and impeding, it can enable the mind to soar, though anchored in the material universe.

Our Lady "pondered in her heart" as she did her chores, and so the Church prays at Prime every day as she gets down to business:

> And let the glorious beauty of the Lord our God be upon us, and direct the work of our hands for us, ... O do Thou direct the work of our hands!

because work is ennobled and raised to a higher plane, made radiant, as it were, by the activity of the mind.

People who despise manual work have poorly cultivated intelligences. Any saint can tell you that. When St. Benedict put in his Rule, "Idleness is the enemy of the soul," he didn't mean just physical idleness, or, being St. Benedict, he would have said so. Mental idleness is just as bad. It's worse, because like ragged underwear, it doesn't show until something vital snaps.

St. Benedict didn't leave his monks' study to chance any more than he left their chores to chance. He stipulated that "the brethren, therefore, must be occupied at stated hours in manual labor, and again at other hours in sacred reading," because he knew perfectly well what would happen if he didn't.

Housewives are no different. A housewife who makes her beds only "when she gets a chance" isn't much of a housekeeper; and a housewife who studies only when she gets a chance doesn't do much studying. St. Benedict suggests extra reading during the afternoon nap. Amended to "during the children's nap," most of us could manage that much. I gather it's not so important that the time be long as that the time be *fixed*, like bed-making, because like bed-making it's a necessary part of daily duty. Besides, if the housewife doesn't do any reading, what is her mind doing while she makes the beds? What is she going to talk about in conversation? The neighbors? (*Touché!*)

Mother Janet Stuart, who wrote probably one of the finest books in the world on the education of young girls, had a lot to say about mental idleness in women and the way we make manual work an excuse for being too lazy to use our minds and develop our inner life. We are told she stoutly maintained that the spiritual classics which thunder against the dangers of too much learning were written for men, that the danger for women lay the other way, in a contented ignorance. Because she was a great educator, she understood that learning has only one real objective: sanctity, and that intellectual and spiritual progress are closely allied.

I wish you would read a letter St. Augustine wrote to a man who made a virtue of taking his religion purely "on faith" without reasoning about it. The saint lambastes him in beautiful, balanced Latin up one side and down the other. "Perish the thought," he wrote, "that we should think He hates in us the very thing in which He created us superior to the other animals! We couldn't even believe if we didn't have reasoning souls!"

St. Augustine's *muttum* was certainly THINK. How he hated that mental sloth which masquerades as humility, that "I know my pore little ole limitations," that "I'm just a housewife!" Ignorance is as much an effect of the Fall as concupiscence and must be battled as ruthlessly.

"Ignorance is the leprosy of the soul," said St. John Rossi. He was a parish priest who didn't come up against any outstanding intellects in his daily rounds. As a matter of fact, his favorite apostolate was among the fallen women of Rome. He just understood that the sin of not using one's mind is a sin whatever your I.Q. Our Lord said we had to produce according to our capacity. It's curious to note in the parable of the talents according to St. Matthew that it's the servant who was given only one talent who hid it in the earth and did nothing with it. It wasn't the servants who were given five or two talents. We get the idea, somehow, that these last could hardly wait to run out and invest them. I suppose our Lord was trying to show us that it's precisely those to whom not much is given who are tempted to do nothing with what little they have, not those who are highly gifted. A giant intellect like St. Augustine's flexes its mental muscles for pure joy. It's real work to exercise a small brain, and it takes solid humility to keep at it.

What's more, Our Lord doesn't sentimentalize about the servant with that one measly talent. In punishment for evading his obligation, his master says, "Take away therefore the talent from him, and give it to him who has the ten talents. ... But as for the unprofitable servant, cast him forth into the darkness outside where there will be the weeping and the gnashing of teeth" *(Matt. 25:28-30)*.

St. Benedict didn't fool around either. His Rule reads:

> But one or two senior monks should certainly be deputed to go round the monastery at the times when the brethren are occupied in reading, to see that there be no slothful brother who spends his time in idleness or gossip [ouch!] and neglects the reading, so that he not only does himself harm but also disturbs others.

If there be such a one (which God forbid), let him be corrected once and a second time; if he does not amend, let him undergo the punishment of the Rule, so that the rest may be afraid.

Before we all rush for our library cards, let me note in passing that what you read is up to you. It's one of the awful choices presented to literate people. It must be fairly obvious that before God a housewife who reads *Raving Romances* doesn't make beds the way a housewife does who reads Swinburne (seriously), or one who feeds on St. Bernard or the Liturgy. All I know is the less time you have for reading, the more solid that reading must be. If you can afford only one set of silver, don't fool with plate. It won't wear. Any housewife knows that.

For a Christian, Scripture is basic reading. Next come books written by saints, because they have the grace of stating great truths simply, so a distracted housewife can grasp them. Also, they don't take themselves too seriously, obscuring the point. Taking oneself too seriously is an effect of pride. Lucifer, the proudest of creatures, takes himself very seriously indeed. Lucifer is an egregious square. Unfortunately, a lot of good reading, like virtue, gets a bad name because for some unaccountable reason it attracts the worst squares. Actually no square ever really gets the hang of virtue, and certainly no square should ever read theology.

God invented humor. It must have been an effect of His mercy. Right after the Fall, taking cognizance of hangdog Adam shorn of all his supernatural gifts, scrunched into the "garments of skin" He had made for him to replace those miserable sewed-up fig leaves, the Lord God said wryly, "Indeed! The man has become one of Us, knowing good and evil!" *(Gen. 3:22).*

So irony was born. It was a bad moment for Adam, but he was offered the inestimable grace of laughing with God at himself if he chose, thereby alleviating his condition several degrees.

Ever since this beginning, God's transcendent irony has been the delight of saints and the torment of sinners. It's God's supreme irony that sends poor little nobody good people to the heights of heaven and rich influential bad people to the depths of hell. That's real humor. It is never recorded that our Lord ever laughed, but His humor pervades the Gospels. Anybody who doesn't bear God's humor in mind when he does spiritual reading is going to let the biggest jokes go right over his head.

I don't know who your favorite authors are for blue Mondays, but I can recommend several theologians who have written a lot about the transfiguration of the body and how it's likely to be in heaven. I gather from them that the main thing that makes my blue Mondays blue is my *crassness*.

Crassness is an attribute of matter that prohibits my sitting the same place you're sitting or being in two or three places at once. It's the real reason I can't go through a closed door with four wastebaskets in hand as I tried to do only this morning.

Not only do I have crassness, but the wastebaskets and everything I pick up have crassness, and that largely makes Monday what it is. This is not a permanent condition, however, say the theologians. In heaven I'll be endowed with subtlety and can flit as I please. I find theologians very cheering, and that's one reason I read them.

For plain laughs, I like to read letters of direction written to duchesses and high-born ladies. When your nails are broken and your nose is red from washing windows on a cold day, and you're feeling pretty sorry for yourself, nothing so restores a sense of proportion as perusing something like the following. It's from Archbishop Fenelon to a hapless lady of the French court:

> Chains of gold are no less chains than those of iron; and while the wearer is an object of envy she is worthy of compassion! ... Some He leads by bitter privations: as to you, He seems to lead you by overwhelming you with the enjoyment of empty prosperity; He makes your lot hard and difficult by dint of those very things which blind outsiders fancy to be the most perfect enjoyment of life! And so He carries on two good works in you, —He teaches you by experience, and causes you to mortify self by the very things which foster evil and wickedness in many men. You are like that king we read of beneath whose hand whatever he touched turned to gold, and whose riches were his misery. ...
>
> God is very ingenious in making crosses for us. Some He makes of lead and iron, which are overwhelming in themselves; and some He makes of straw, which seem so light and yet are no less heavy to bear: others He makes of gold and jewels, the glitter of which dazzles those around and excites the world's envy, but which all the while are as crucifying as the most despised of crosses. He makes us crosses of whatever we love best, and turns all to bitterness. High position involves constraint and harass. ...

Well, window washing involves a lot of high position, too, but I don't have to wear my gold and jewels. You see, there's always something to be thankful for!

X. HEN IN AN AIRPLANE or CLUCK, CLUCK

"Cheer up, girls. It could be worse. You could be married!" These may not be the exact words St. Teresa used in the *Way of Perfection* to encourage her Carmelite nuns to greater patience in small sufferings, but that's the gist in modern American. If you don't believe she said that, you can look it up. It's in Chapter 12 of her book.

I hope you do, because there's a lot of sound practical advice in that book, for nuns and housewives alike. Many of St. Teresa's relatives, whose homes she had occasion to visit, were married and she spoke from the ringside.

There was something else St. Teresa said about lay life, and the first time I came across it, it made me pretty mad. As I remember, it was in her *Autobiography*. She was congratulating her nuns on being nuns because in the married state, said she, a person travels to perfection "at the pace of a hen." I don't think any phrase in all spiritual literature ever spurred me on to greater efforts. Saints, I kept telling myself, are not infallible. St. Teresa could be wrong about this, without any detraction whatever to her sanctity.

Well, to make a long story short, have you ever watched a hen hurry? It's the funniest sight in the world. She squawks and flaps and stretches her neck, and when she lengthens her stride too far, she topples over. To maintain any dignity at all, a hen must keep her pace henly, cluck serenely, and peck daintily, simply because she's a hen. I am a hen, but admitting it hasn't been easy.

I never saw the point about being a hen until I had this dream about airplanes: I was cruising around about 30,000 feet up, seated quite comfortably with the family around me, lots of baggage, magazines and other passengers about. There was a pilot and I guess a co-pilot doing the important work in the nose of the plane, while I was amusing the children and talking to my husband in the cabin. I looked out the window to admire the clouds when to my consternation I saw a man swinging out all alone in a tiny seat at the end of a long rope hanging from another plane going in the same direction as ours. He was reading a book.

"Good grief!" I exclaimed, "I'm certainly glad I don't have to travel that way. I'd be scared to death!"

At that point somebody made me get up and walk to the rear of our plane, where a large door was thrown open, and I was made to walk to the edge and look down. I think I gasped. It was a very vivid dream.

"Look, you have just as much reason to be scared to death as that man has," the unknown person said. "You're just as high up, and just as dependent on the airplane as he is. Don't let your surroundings fool you. All that baggage and all those people don't change the essentials of your position at all." With that I woke up.

I'm no Daniel. Maybe I should stick to the "I know a housewife who" formula, because now I see it has its advantages. Without arguing the dangers or merits of dreams, let me just say that this one cleared up quite a few points about hens in no way contrary to sound doctrine.

I suppose the man dangling out by himself was a Carthusian or some other kind of austere religious. He might have been one of St. Teresa's nuns. Anyway, he had some special brand of courage. He was flying high, fast, and alone. He must have been aware at all times of his position, his dependence on the plane, and his rope. Other than his book, he had no distractions to keep him occupied with anything but his destination.

Now the interior of a passenger plane is definitely for hens, or ladies in lay life. For hens who would rather fly high, alone, and perilously, it's rather a humiliating way to travel and therefore good for a henly soul with high-falutin' ideas. She travels in the company of others, though maybe she'd rather be alone, occupied by small duties, comforts and distractions of which she may or may not avail herself as she pleases. Her destination, however, remains the same as the Carthusian's, for her destination is God. Her means of reaching her destination is the same as his: an airplane, which we can call grace. This airplane in both cases is piloted, let us say by the usual pilots, the priests according to the order of Melchisedech.

Before the analogy breaks down, as it must eventually, let's just point out again that the *essentials* of religious and lay life in no way differ. The great means of reaching God in no way differ. These are always prayer, Mass and the Sacraments, the great channels of grace.

Perhaps instead of calling the airplane grace, we could simply call it Christ, because He is all means. Only by Him can we stay aloft, or travel or ever reach our goal. He carries us, all the way. The Little Flower called Him *l'ascenseur divin*, the divine elevator.

Once we've decided on our destination and bought our ticket, what little we do on our journey boils down to what goes on inside the passenger plane, or on that little free-flying seat. And here, the main thing is not hindering the flight, and staying put as much as possible. This means mostly doing the obvious.

If the Carthusian doesn't stay put, he'll know it right away. If he drops his book (probably Scripture), he'll miss it immediately. The poor hen is surrounded by lots of books and magazines. She can even get up and change her seat if she likes, or walk around a little, but that doesn't change the direction in which she travels. She has many duties the man in the flying seat doesn't have: seeing that the children behave and are properly clothed for the journey, teaching them something about where they're going, making the trip as pleasant as possible for her husband and the other passengers, perhaps giving comfort to someone sick or old.

She also has lots of little temptations to avoid, and bewildering little choices to make about seemingly unimportant things. She can read a movie magazine or a travel book; she can play cards or snooze or meditate when the children are quiet; she can take an aspirin for her headache or not; she can read the children a story or engage a stranger in conversation; or she can retire to the cocktail lounge and get herself pleasantly blotto. She could take an overdose of sleeping pills and be pronounced dead on arrival. These little choices presented constantly to her free will are what constitute, I think, the "pace of a hen" that St. Teresa was talking about. The housewife can't avoid them. They are the very stuff of her existence, her spiritual building blocks.

For the Carthusian, these are eliminated in one fell swoop. It's true, he flies exposed like an eagle straight to God. That's his special vocation. But the housewife's is no less special, just because there are lots of housewives and relatively few Carthusians. She is meant to sanctify a whole lifetime of seemingly meaningless details, to pick and choose among them and make them serve the end to which she and the other passengers are travelling. She must use for her sanctification the very things the religious is privileged to give up in order to accomplish his. For her, these little details are the stuff of the "little way" which the Little Flower—presumably a high flyer like our Carthusian—came to tell us about.

She was divinely enlightened concerning the fantastic progress to be made at the pace of a hen, and used no other pace herself. She achieved sanctity at record speed, dying transformed in God's love at twenty-four, and left a blueprint of spirituality for the whole modern world. Her life was singularly devoid of visions and ecstasies and was spent almost entirely in doing the obvious perfectly, and without calling attention to herself. She succeeded so well, one of her sisters in religion wondered what could be found to say about her in the death notice to be circulated about her within the Order.

Not that this idea is entirely original with her. As our Lord made plain: "Every scribe instructed in the kingdom of heaven is like a householder who brings forth from his storeroom things new and old" *(Matt. 13:52).*

Doing the small and obvious well has never been easy. Though it doesn't make exciting reading, it has always been the daily bread of saints. St. Francis de Sales put it this way in his *Introduction to the Devout Life*:

> We must fight great temptations with invincible courage, ... yet, to fight well against small temptations may be more profitable still. Though great temptations may surpass them in quality, small temptations are far more numerous and so the victory over them is comparable. Wolves and bears are obviously more dangerous than flies yet they are less irritating and do not try our patience to the same extent.

Inasmuch as one of the good Bishop's favorite little mortifications was letting the flies crawl over his bald head unhindered, he can't be accused of improvising! He continues:

> It is easy to refrain from murder but hard to refrain from the anger which we are constantly tempted to express; ... easy to avoid stealing but hard to avoid envy; easy to avoid perjury but hard to avoid lying; easy never to get drunk yet hard always to be temperate; easy not to wish the death of another but hard never to wish him harm; easy never to defame him but hard never to despise him.

Easy to take a flying leap now and then, but difficult to poke along at the pace of a hen.

The Jesuit Father Jean Grou, also a great director of souls, has something to say too about those deceptively "little" things. He spent the latter part of his life living with an English family whose members he directed, so he is particularly aware of the problems of the laity. In Father Grou's *Manual for Interior Souls*, we find the following passage:

> And our Lord Jesus Christ said, *He that is faithful in that which is least, shall be faithful also in that which is greatest....* Properly speaking, there is nothing either little or great with regard to the things of God. Everything that bears the impress of His Will is great, however small it may be in itself. ... It is only the Will of God which gives any value to things.
>
> In the same way, with regard to our sanctification, such and such a thing, which appears to us very little in itself, may be of so great consequence, that our perfection, and even our salvation, may depend upon it. God attaches His grace to what pleases Him; we cannot know of ourselves what may be the good or evil consequences of any single action which seems to us of little importance. Of what grace may I be deprived if I neglect it? What grace may come to me if I perform it? This is just what I do not know; and in this uncertainty a constant and exact fidelity to grace is the only course to pursue. ...
>
> And if the death of self-love is more gradual, it is none the less sure, for the constant practice of little things reduces it to such a state of weakness that at last it has no power of reviving: therefore, it is generally in this way that God finishes our self-love.

But never mind, Scripture promises the race isn't to the swift. St. Teresa never said that hen didn't get there!

XI. THE INSIDE STORY

For cloistered contemplatives and caged canaries, *cella continuata dulcescit*. This is a phrase well known to the former and easily illustrated by the latter. It means roughly "Stay home and love it." A really mature, well-adjusted canary won't leave his cage unless forced out, and the holiest contemplative keeps to his cell unless duty drives him from it. The author of *The Imitation of Christ* tells us, "Your cell will become dear to you if you remain in it, but if you do not, it will become wearisome."

What I'm leading up to is that good housewives stay home. There's nothing, absolutely nothing, that makes you hate the house and everything in it as being continually out of it. Don't ask me why. I just know from experience that this is so. I confess it took me longer than most people to find this out, but eventually, it sank in. Staying home, let me hasten to inject, doesn't mean never leaving the premises. It just means staying home.

The Holy Spirit, it would seem, likes women who stay home. In the Book of Proverbs, divine Wisdom is pictured for us as a woman who enjoys keeping within her own four walls:

> Wisdom hath built herself a house, she hath hewn her out seven pillars.
> She hath slain her victims, mingled her wine, and set forth her table.
> She hath sent her maids [never going out herself if she can send somebody else]
> to invite to the tower and the walls of the city:
> Whosoever is a little one, let him come to me *(Prov. 9:1-4)*.

Wisdom likes company and loves to entertain "little ones," but does it in her own home. Folly, on the other hand, is shown as a housewife who "just can't stand being cooped up any longer," and is always looking for fun on the outside:

> A foolish woman and clamorous, and full of allurements, and knowing nothing at all,
> Sat at the door of her house, upon a seat, in a high place of the city,

65

> To call them that pass by the way and to the fool she said, Stolen waters
> are sweeter, and hidden bread is more pleasant *(Prov. 9:13-17)*.

Folly's home, definitely, is the place she goes to when all the
other joints are closed.

Here again, St. Benedict had all this very well figured out,
along with the other things. Besides the usual vows of poverty,
chastity and obedience, he introduced a vow of stability. This
means his monks promised to stay put. Sound psychologist that he
was, St. Benedict put an end at the beginning to all those thoughts
of "I'd serve God a lot better somewhere else," and a great deal of
fruitless looking over the fence at the greener grass.

A formal vow of this kind would be wonderful for housewives
who can't stop gadding, or who are sure they could serve humanity
better if they had "wider scope for their talents" outside the
confines of their homes.

Father Thomas Merton, who lives under a rule based on St.
Benedict's, has this to stay about stability in his book, *The Sign of
Jonas*:

> The limitations of the monk [read housewife, or anybody], and the
> limitations of the community he lives in, form a part of God's plan for the
> sanctification both of individuals and communities. ... This [vow] implies a
> deep act of faith: the recognition that it does not much matter where we are
> or whom we live with, provided we can devote ourselves to prayer, enjoy a
> certain amount of silence, poverty and solitude, work with our hands, read
> and study the things of God, and above all love one another as Christ has
> loved us.

Throughout the centuries, the greatest minds and biggest
pocketbooks of the Church have conspired to contrive monastic
establishments which by rule and architecture would provide
special souls with these elements of human living of which Father
Merton speaks, and which lead most directly to God.

All are the housewife's for the asking. Solitude? Silence? I can
hear you laughing. But wait. Solitude doesn't mean being a hermit,
as we have seen. Solitude means being alone. It means being alone
the way a monk is alone at refectory, the way a commuter is alone
waiting for a bus, the way a mother is alone doing the family
washing, or listening, half-groggy, to the prattle of a three-year-

old. Nobody can deny housework is lonely. That's one of its most trying aspects and is responsible for more bridge games, coffee klatches, misguided charity and jobs outside the home than any of us would care to own up to.

We're often accused of talking too much, but that's only when we get the chance, and somebody happens to be listening. Most of the day we live under a rule of silence far stricter and more inexorable than do many religious orders. For hours we may be silent and alone physically to a degree many monks dream of but are never granted.

This silence and solitude, aiding and abetting the mysterious interaction of manual labor and study on the soul, is supposed to produce the highest prayer. St. Benedict hardly mentions prayer in his Rule. He gives no little rules on how to go about it, because he takes it for granted that the entire big Rule exists only to keep it going "without ceasing."

"It would be a bad business if we could pray only alone in corners," said St. Teresa. Nobody knows this better than the housewife. For her, *constant prayer* is about the only possible prayer. As St. Jeanne de Chantal's servants put it when she acquired St. Francis de Sales as her director,

> Oh, things are much better now! With Madame's previous director, she was always upsetting the household with her prayer times, but now Madame prays all the time and doesn't bother anybody.

St. Jeanne was a housewife who eventually got herself canonized, so we have to admit the problem boils down to whether a housewife really wants to take advantage of her opportunities and whether she truly seeks God. For women who can't or won't take it, there's always a radio to turn up. There's always one more club to join, friends to badger, useless shopping for hats that will end up on a table at the rummage sale, dull television programs, day dreams and whiskey.

Solitude, God knows, isn't for sissies. It's for God. It's also for brain-washing, incorrigible criminals—and saints. There must be a lot of good to be gotten from it, because it draws devils like nobody's business. The demon *acedia*, for instance. *Acedia* is a Greek word (I just can't help it) which means "couldn't care less—

to hell with it," and that's where this demon hopes you'll go, of course. He was well known to the desert fathers as the devil whose specialty is excruciating boredom, relentlessly driving his victim into the alleviating distractions of the world. He was considered one of the worst. Someday I hope to find a housewife who hasn't met up with him!

Then there's the noonday devil, who specializes in making black look white. He's the "devastating plague at noon" who strikes you down in broad daylight, tempting you to evil under the semblance of obvious good. He leads you to mind the neighbors' business by telling you to "take an interest in people and the world around you." Stop all that religious reading and don't pray so much, he says. You're not a saint! You'll go nuts! Your health will suffer.

"You'll be like God," he told Mother Eve, offering her that fruit. That certainly seemed like an awfully good idea. Women just naturally like to better themselves. Don't underestimate him. The Church doesn't. For centuries she has prayed every Sunday night for help against this *daemonio meridiana*, when praying Psalm 90. This Psalm was quoted by Satan when he tempted Our Lord during His forty days in the desert. He's scared to death of people who don't mind being alone on occasion.

But devils aren't the only thing a housewife contends with at home alone. Like everybody else, she's got the world and the flesh. She can let her children go to that party she disapproves of, because the "right people" are there. She can buy a mink coat she can't afford. She can keep nibbling between meals. She can let dinner burn and write a book ... telling other housewives how to live.

You and I know being alone in a house day after day can be awful. It's like dirt. You have to make it work *for* you, because it won't stay neutral. When you're alone, God's voice can be heard very clearly, and one's defects have a way of coming to mind. The thoughts that arise in solitude show us to ourselves and give us no quarter. As I say, it can be awful.

Without God, nobody can stand solitude long. And nobody stands solitude long without coming up against Him. When we come up against Him, we want to possess Him, and that's when the *cella* begins to *dulcescit*, "The cell grows sweet." Prayer grows.

And nothing so enlarges the confines of the house as praying in it. It's like Ezechiel's vision. He saw a little house which from the outside measured only "six cubits and a handbreadth," but once he got inside, it took him some 200 verses to describe and measure all the rooms and porches and thresholds he finds in it—most of them larger than the house itself. It's that mysterious "handbreadth" that contains infinite dimension. That handbreadth, the mystics tell us, is prayer.

It's at this point and not before, that a housewife really begins to be a housewife, and not just a housekeeper for a lot of relatives. "She hath hewn her out seven pillars." She has now erected the support for her sanctification, her faith strengthened by the seven gifts of the Holy Ghost. She begins to stand as spokesman before God for the microcosm before her: her home. Without her voice of praise, all the things around her are mute before their Creator: the sofa pillows, the flowers on the table, the pictures on the wall, even the goldfish going *pop! pop!* in their bowl. As Adam spoke for the material universe when God told him to name the creatures, so the housewife, in her life of prayer, speaks for the little universe given to her "to till and to keep." This duty of prayer and praise is of the same nature as that performed by the contemplative orders in singing the Divine Office. It is the *Opus Dei*, the work of God, and basically, of course, the duty of every human being.

It hit me like a ton of bricks to discover that washing children's faces and cooking meals are elements, not of an active life, but of a contemplative life. Housewives are contemplatives. That's what this book is all about, really. They are contemplatives in the same large sense that woman is the contemplative sex. She nourishes from her being, rather than by her actions, as do men. Our Lady, Queen of Contemplation, was a housewife, and I refuse to consider this a mere coincidence.

The Little Flower said she wanted to perform all roles in the Church. She wanted to be a missionary, a catechist, a nurse, a preacher, a martyr, everything. In order to fill them all, she took up the life of a contemplative. Now, the housewife is the natural figure of contemplation. She isn't a priest, but she may rear a priest. She isn't a nurse, but her daughter may decide to be one. There is no vocation in the Church which she can't foster, even on the visible level.

The mother bears the same relation to the rest of the family that the contemplative orders bear to the rest of the Church. These make fruitful the activity of the Church by hidden lives of prayer and penance. By staying in one place they send apostles to Zanzibar. They avert disasters. If Sodom had had ten contemplatives, it wouldn't have been destroyed.

As her husband is the channel of authority under God, the housewife is the channel of nourishing grace. As the husband is the head of the family, the Church teaches that the mother is the heart. He rears the children mainly by the exercise of authority; she governs them mainly by the force of her prayer. This doesn't mean he doesn't pray, or she doesn't spank. What I'm trying to say is that a housewife rooted in God distributes grace with the breakfast cereal, and her "vow of stability" is the nexus of the home.

The Mother Superior of a French secular institute once told me, "Whatever you do, don't try to lead a spiritual life alone"; and she cited the failure of the priest workers in France, who hadn't taken the precaution of living in community among atheist populations. Man is cenobitic by nature. Every human being must have a continuing source of spiritual replenishment. For religious, it's the convent; for laymen, it must be the home. Into both the grace of Mass, prayer, and the sacraments must pour as into a reservoir from which all can draw, not just now and then, but constantly.

Most husbands go out to work. Children go to school. It's only the housewife who gets a chance to stay home and lead a contemplative life. Often she is the only member of the family who can represent them at Mass during the week. If she can't mind the reservoir, she condemns them to thirst of a special kind. This is very hard for me to put into words. Luckily, my husband has helped me out with a quotation from St. John Chrysostom, who wasn't called "golden-mouthed" for nothing. In one of his sermons to the laity of Antioch, he puts it very well indeed:

> The husband engaged at the Agora and Courts of Justice, is torn by exterior conflicts. But the wife seated in her home as in a school of philosophy [sic!], her mind turned inwards, will be able to devote herself to prayer and reading and with what time remains, to wisdom.

I remind you this is St. John speaking, not I:

> And as those who dwell in the desert are undisturbed by others, so also is the wife who enjoys perpetual calm within the interior of the home. If by chance she must needs go out, this should not trouble her. To come to the assembly here, or to go to the baths [supermarkets ?], she must necessarily leave her house; but as a rule she remains indoors. There she can philosophize at leisure and relieve her husband's troubled mind on his return, drive away his vain worrying thoughts and the evil effects of the outer world by filling his mind with the good things of home.

See?

Now, if you'll excuse me, I have to call up somebody about a second hand snare drum. Tavy has just joined the school band, and says he has to start practicing right away.

XII. CATS IN THE PRESENT MOMENT

As far as I know, no housecat is mentioned in all of Scripture.[3] Dogs, pigs, lions, snakes, bulls, horses, gnats, whales, yes. Even geckos. In Leviticus, the Jews are forbidden to eat geckos.

I've seen many a gecko, which is a lizard who says, believe it or not, "Gecko!" He is black and viperish, has suction pads on his feet and hangs, usually head down with his mouth open like a gargoyle, around drainpipes in tropical climes. Housewives come across lots of odd things in their living rooms over the world, and he was one of my oddest. Only beyond the brink of actual starvation would I be tempted to eat him.

I wouldn't eat cats either, but more from respect; for although the Bible never mentions them, I must confess they have played a certain role in my spiritual life, besides being invaluable props for teaching the children the facts of life. Not that I've ever had much direct communication with cats. The only person I know who's had any words with them is Crane. He is our first born son and looks a lot like his name, especially in the legs.

When he was three years old, we had a cat called Jojo. Even more than most cats, this Jojo was forever wanting to go either in or out the front door. Even at his tender age, Crane found him exasperating. When he was on the outside, Jojo learned to knock on the door by flapping the brass mail slot until somebody inside couldn't stand it any longer. As soon as the door was open, in he'd come. But going out was different. He'd just sit and look at the door. If somebody opened it, sometimes he'd go out. Sometimes he wouldn't. If he was forced out, he'd start flapping that slot right away.

---

[3] This is just plain not true. A cloistered friend tells me there is *one* reference to cats in Scripture: Baruch 6:21, where they appear very much in character, leaping onto the heads of idols!

Jojo was sitting looking at the front door one afternoon. I was resting my feet on the sofa, expecting Lydia to be born in a few weeks. Risking disaster, I ignored Jojo. He was impossible.

At this point Crane came along, dragging a wooden train. The door was pretty heavy for him, and he'd gotten pretty tired of opening for Jojo just to have him sit there. He was a very grave, serene child, given to very few words. Almost as few as the cat. He mulled over the situation, staring at the animal fixedly. "Look, Jojo," he said finally, looking him straight in the eye, "if you *weally* want to go out, say; meow! meow!"

Jojo stood up, waved his tail and said, "Meow! Meow!" Crane immediately walked to the door, tugged at it with all his might, and out Jojo walked, tail in air. Crane closed the door. Neither of them ever changed expression. For a minute, they had me. "Now, why didn't I think of that?" I wondered idly.

Then it hit me. I looked at Crane. He was playing with his train again, utterly oblivious of anything unusual, I was what is known as an agnostic at the time, and believe me, a situation like this for an agnostic can be especially baffling. Without the faith, many must come to mental breakdown when confronted by animals and children combined.

"Crane" I began. But it was no use. Mystery is mystery, and a home reeks with it.

There was so much I couldn't explain, why quibble at this? I couldn't bear to tell him cats don't talk, because actually, I don't really know that. To this day, all I can say is they don't talk to me, and what's that to Crane, if they talk to him? Hang it all, any cat can say "Meow! Meow!" when he wants to. Any three-year-old knows that. I could no more tell Crane about cats than I could tell him about God, not knowing for sure.

Jojo is now long dead, much mourned, and buried among the irises behind the stable. Crane laughs when I tell this story today, because he's grown up, and that's what grown-ups are supposed to do at stories like that. For all I know, however, he can still talk to cats and maybe he does, privately. He talks little to people. We all agree he has a way with animals, because he's the only member of the family the mare won't bite, and he had a pig who used to follow him regularly into the house to be petted. We have lots of animal stories in the family, and except for the time the bird tried to nest in Lydia's hair, most of them involve Crane.

After I found out about God, animals didn't seem so mysterious, though children still baffle me. Cats, however, are something special. On one desperate occasion, I remember taking a cat named Mohair for my spiritual director. Don't be shocked. It was on very good authority, as I shall show.

I had been reading some manual of the spiritual life—perhaps the one by Rev. Tanquerey—which stressed, as all such good works must, the absolute necessity of a director to help one avoid the pitfalls on the road to perfection. On checking up right now, I see Rev. Tanquerey quotes an authority, Father Godinez, to prove his point:

> Under God they [directors] are the pilots that conduct souls through this unknown ocean of the spiritual life. If no science, no art, how simple soever, can be learned well without a master, much less can anyone learn this high wisdom of evangelical perfection, wherein such great mysteries are found. This is the reason why I hold it morally impossible that a soul could without a miracle or without a master go through what is highest and most arduous in the spiritual life, without running the risk of perishing.

St. Bernard put it more succinctly: "Whoever teaches himself has a fool for a teacher."

St. Francis de Sales has special praise for the "many good souls ... who in order to subject themselves more perfectly to God, have submitted their will to that of His servants."

In our times, Cardinal Newman urgently counselled spiritual direction for laymen:

> We should all of us be saved a great deal of suffering of various kinds, if we could but persuade ourselves, that we are not the best judges, whether of our own condition, or of God's will toward us. What sensible person undertakes to be his own physician? Yet are the diseases of the mind less intricate, less subtle than those of the body? Is experience of no avail in things spiritual as well as in things material? Does induction lose its office, and science its supremacy, when the soul is concerned? What an inconsistent age is this! Every department of things that are, is pronounced to be capable of science, to rest upon principles, to require teaching, to exercise the reason, except self-discipline. Self-discipline is to take its

chance; it is not to be learned, but it can be performed by each man for himself by a sort of natural instinct. ...

All the saints without exception agree that doing what you please is disastrous. You fall into pride and all your favorite sins, besides never acquiring any real self-knowledge. I couldn't have been easier to convince, but what was I to do? The fact remained that I lived six miles from nowhere in a highly non-Catholic part of the south.

St. Teresa, who had a particular horror of doing her own will, says that although you may search, you will never find out the will of God so assuredly, as by the way of this humble obedience. Somewhere else she said that if you can't find anybody else to obey, well then, "Obey the cat!"

At this precise point in my life when I was floundering most and staring at the ceiling, being literally unable to find anyone at all to "direct" me in my hinterland, there was a scratching at the door. I opened, and Mohair (etymological note: at Mohair's birth, one of the children said, "She needs mo' hair!" Ergo ...) walked in.

Naturally, I remembered St. Teresa.

"Okay, Mo," I said. "What'll it be?" (Always clowning!)

I should have known. Mohair walked immediately over to a rug I had hooked with my own hands. She stretched neck and tail, blinked once or twice, and regurgitated four or five half-digested field mice in a neat little pile in the very middle of the rug. She then jumped into the nearest easy chair and prepared to snooze.

She had just taught me, as only a cat could, the Sacrament of the Present Moment.

What opportunity for the practice of virtue! Saints may have had lepers' sores to kiss, but I had been vouchsafed Mohair! First, resist the urge to pick up said Mohair and throw her out. Then, resist saying interiorly, "Is it for this you learned the conjugation of γίγνομαι?" Next, clean up the mess with as little breath-holding as prudent, to overcome proud fastidiousness, reminding myself I am a sinner and deserve no better. And finally, offer up the whole operation for my sins and those of the world, *lovingly.*

It doesn't do to kid with the saints too much. St. Teresa certainly made her point that afternoon. You can bet I never asked Mohair to direct me again.

Now, no one will question the fact that a good priest with much experience of souls and sound common sense is infinitely superior to a cat in leading one to perfection. St. Francis de Sales, again, tells us that if we pray assiduously and humbly for a good director, God will surely send us one eventually. Until that happens, however, we must face facts. Often circumstances beyond our control are against us. Most parish priests are sadly overworked. Many souls live in inaccessible spots, or their way of life precludes any regular interviews with a director. Outside large cities, very often a suitable director with time at his disposal is simply not to be found.

There's nothing left to do but take St. Francis' advice and pray hard. Then while you wait, take St. Teresa's advice and obey the cat. To mix a metaphor, Obey the Cat at the Pace of a Hen! I'm serious. This obeying the cat entails (no pun intended) breaking one's own will and uniting it to God's by constantly falling in with the demands of the here and now. Father de Caussade, one of the greatest spiritual directors, first coined the phrase "sacrament of the present moment" which Mohair presented so dramatically. It is, par excellence, the layman's sacrament, and God's will is always to be found in it. We may not know God's will for us tomorrow, but we always know what it is at any *actual* moment, simply because it *is*. It's so obvious, it's easily missed.

Besides the fortuitous (whatever that is) events of the day, God makes his will known to us at every moment through the Commandments, the laws of the Church, and the commands of superiors. For the housewife, superiors are mainly her husband, her Bishop or her pastor, and the civil authority. (Minding the speed limit is an inescapable part of perfection.) God also makes His will known to her in her daily duties. Accomplishing these assiduously at the proper time to the best of her ability, without complaint, for pure love of God, automatically places her in God's presence. Essentially, this is prayer.

St. Teresa tells us she often found God among the pots and pans. A pan to be scoured can be God's will for us at a given moment. At that moment, for us, He is there and only there. To leave the pan in the sink and go looking for Him even in church would get us nowhere compared to the grace of scouring the pan, because it's in the pan that duty, or God's will, lies.

When the pan is scoured, or most likely before, the doorbell may ring. Answering it promptly is partaking of the Sacrament of the Present Moment, even if we're dying to answer it. It might be the cat! To keep on scouring the pan now is no good. God's will is now in answering the doorbell.

Whatever it is, doing consistently what is presented to us to do, or not doing what is not presented to us, is a large part of holiness. The experts usually call this "Abandonment to Divine Providence," and a more exciting way to live can't be imagined. This is one case where being a really abandoned woman pays off, and of all women, housewives should be the most abandoned.

Father de Caussade wrote a whole book called *Abandonment to Divine Providence* and begins it thus:

> God continues to speak today as He spoke in former times to our fathers when there were no directors as at present, nor any regular method of direction. ... Then, for those who led a spiritual life, each moment brought some duty to be faithfully accomplished. Their whole attention was thus concentrated consecutively like a hand that marks the hours which, at each moment, traverses the space allotted to it. Their minds, incessantly activated by the impulsion of divine grace, turned imperceptibly to each new duty that presented itself by the permission of God at different hours of the day. Such were the hidden springs by which the conduct of Mary was actuated. Mary was the most simple of all creatures, and the most closely united to God. Her answer to the angel when she said: "Fiat mihi secundum verbum tuum": contained all the mystic theology of her ancestors to whom everything was reduced, as it is now, to the purest, simplest submission of the soul to the will of God, under whatever form it presents itself. ...
>
> There are remarkably few extraordinary characteristics in the outward events of the life of the most holy Virgin. ... Her exterior life is represented as very ordinary and simple. She did and suffered the same things that anyone in a similar state of life might do or suffer. She goes to visit her cousin Elizabeth as her other relatives did. She took shelter in a stable in consequence of her poverty. She returned to Nazareth from whence she had been driven by the persecution of Herod, and lived there with Jesus and Joseph, supporting themselves by the work of their hands. It was in this way that the holy family gained their daily bread. But what a divine nourishment Mary and Joseph received from this daily bread for the strengthening of

their faith! It is like a sacrament to sanctify all their moments. What treasures of grace lie concealed in these moments filled, apparently, by the most ordinary events. That which is visible might happen to anyone, but the invisible, discerned by faith, is no less than God operating very great things.

O Bread of Angels! Heavenly manna! Pearl of the Gospel! SACRAMENT OF THE PRESENT MOMENT! Thou givest God under as lowly a form as the manger, the hay, or the straw. And to whom dost thou give Him? "Esurientes implevit bonis." God reveals Himself to the humble under the most lowly forms. …

Do you suppose the Holy Family kept a cat?

XIII. BEING SIMPLY MORTIFIED

I remember once discussing suitable forms of penance in a seminary in the Far East. (Housewives, you are reminded, can infiltrate anywhere.) The Rector was warning me about the dangers of indiscriminate fasting in that part of the tropics, where Western appetites often flag and fasting has to be done in reverse, just to keep one going.

"Now don't cut down on food," he said, "just practice some very *simple* mortification, my child." He looked off into space for an instant and returned with, "For instance, just don't drink any water."

It was a very, very hot day. I must have turned a shade pale, because he added enthusiastically, by way of clinching the sale, "That's a very good mortification, you know, because no one ever notices!" (That, indeed, is true. Soda pop, cocktails, fruit punch, coffee, tea, beer, wine, kickapoo joy juice or love potions are bound to be forced on you at one time or another, but water, never!)

If any homebodies are tempted to doubt the caliber of Catholic priests sent out to the mission field, let me hasten to add that this Rector, an Argentinian, was not one to preach what he didn't practice. We had him to dinner not long after this, and I watched him quite shamelessly through three courses and the coffee and brandy. It was the brandy that really earned him my respect. This "simple mortification" I happen to know wasn't exactly original with him. St. Philip Neri liked it too. I know he prescribed it once to a hopeless drunkard.

"Drink all the wine you want," the saint told him cheerfully, "just no water." Don't worry, the drunkard was cured in a week, because there's nothing like alcohol to make you thirsty ... and nothing like a saint's prayers to effect a conversion.

I'm afraid this mortification proved rather too simple for me. I distinctly remember looking on perspiration as a hopeless luxury to be avoided at all costs. If you want to get a taste of the Rector's simple suggestion sometime, just try doing without water some hot Fourth of July, watching a parade, drinking lots of beer and pop and eating hot dogs smothered in mustard, and you'll get an inkling, but only an inkling, of what it's like near the Equator. And it's true no one ever notices. As I said, water is one beverage you can refuse or leave in your glass any time without causing the slightest comment. Nobody ever presses on you one more glass of water "for the road."

I'll never forget that Rector, nor the point he drove home. Doing without the water, of course, wasn't the point. The real point was that the most crucifying mortifications, and the best for you, are those that are so simple they cut to the roots of you while escaping all notice. A housewife's life bristles with them. She's a fool not to use them. Throwing away that kind of wealth is worse than throwing out a good hambone or letting fruit spoil. Not just her family suffers; the whole Mystical Body is deprived.

At the risk of being "negative" —anybody who doesn't concentrate on offering up joys and consolations these days gets this from the *avant-garde*—may we ask who doesn't need to do penance? Who doesn't need to keep in training? Who doesn't have some obligation to save some soul besides his own? Penance is a commodity the whole world needs desperately. At Fatima the Blessed Virgin asked it specifically of three children. To let one of the major sources of supply—the harried housewife—go to waste is calamitous.

I'm not going to mention all the obvious forms like boring chores, whimpering children, flat tires, stubbed toes and stopped-up sinks. Any woman who consistently goes through these cheerful and smiling for any length of time is bound to be noticed. Anyone serious about the spiritual life tries to offer these up as a matter of course, or at least feels guilty about not doing it. If there's an audience, you'll probably be admired. That's bad for you and takes half the good out of the mortification. If there isn't an audience, you may end up admiring yourself, and that's worse. So keep a close watch on yourself.

When God wrote the laywoman's rule for Mother Eve, it wasn't in any permanent form. He revises it for every generation and every individual, though its main outlines remain the same.

Nor does He omit any of the little niceties such as He gives to her sisters under the skin in the cloister. They're just extraordinarily ordinary. The housewife doesn't ordinarily wear a hair shirt, lest it be noticed and cause comment (I guess), but she's welcome any time to the equally effective and quite excruciating torment of a scratchy sweater. If your sweater can help your spiritual life as it helps you look chic, let it! I don't own a hair shirt, but I have a scratchy, stylish sweater that's a dilly.

Then too, if you can't stick to a diet, try fasting. Only remember in public to call it dieting. Very few women can stick to diets because, frankly, a good figure just isn't worth that kind of agony. But for the love of God and a special intention, with all the fat housewives in Heaven helping, anything is possible! The soul you save may be your own, and the good figure is a happy by-product, which is all a good figure should ever be.

This goes for fancy shoes that pinch, heavy earrings that hurt, and maybe even a second helping of gooey dessert you hate but accept just to please the hostess. The most salutary part of this type of mortification is that it strikes at not just plain pride, but spiritual pride. To the casual observer—if you have any—you have the added humiliation of appearing vain, fashionable, or plain gluttonous, if you appear anything.

This is rather the quintessence of our Lord's admonition,

> And when you fast, do not look gloomy like the hypocrites, who disfigure their faces in order to appear to men as fasting. Amen I say to you, they have received their reward.
> But thou, when thou dost fast, anoint thy head and wash thy face, so that thou mayest not be seen fasting by men, but by thy Father, who is in secret; and thy Father, who sees in secret, will reward thee *(Matt. 6:16-18)*.

No nun ever gets the opportunities to disguise penances that the housewife does. One of the most telling mortifications for proud souls, especially bluestockings, is being conventional. Just wearing a hat to a tea party, for instance, for one who is above hats, is marvelous for humility. If the hat is fancy and ridiculous, it's even better. Frankly, I can't imagine a humiliation to equal putting some of the flouncier creations on one's head, where it can be seen by all. Of course, if you like fancy hats, try a plain one next season.

If you pride yourself on your wit and generally keep your entourage convulsed, learn to come out with such killers as "Yes, that's very true," or "Of course, there are two sides to every question," or "I guess it's the atom bomb that causes all this crazy weather." Not all the time, of course, or you may not be invited again, and your active apostolate will languish, but just enough to keep you from spreading yourself.

Parties, where the "apostolate of presence" can be carried on if nothing else, lend themselves especially well to this sort of thing. If you like easy chairs, pick out a straight one. Better still, if you like straight ones, pick out a squashy one and pass for lazy. Or you can sidle up to the worst bore of the evening and really listen to him, with love in your heart. This last, I realize, is for advanced souls, but practice makes perfect here as elsewhere ... I'm told.

Certainly a great part of a woman's penitential life lies precisely in such circumstances: where everybody else feels she must be having herself a whale of a time. (I'll mortify myself right here and not expatiate on Thanksgiving Dinner.) St. Francis de Sales explains this much better than I can in his famous *Introduction to the Devout Life*, written for a lady in society. The knack of making spiritual hay from the simple and obvious, all the while remaining pleasant and hidden in plain sight like the purloined letter is a virtuosity especially proper to the lay saint.

"Mais assurément," I can hear the holy Bishop say, "of course, dear lady, play cards all night if you feel you must. Just do not neglect to pray all the time!"

God knows all vigils aren't kept in church, because God doesn't want it that way. Young mothers don't get up in the middle of the night like Carmelites to sing Matins, but they get up in the middle of the night to feed the baby, who frequently sings Matins, Lauds and Vespers too. As we've noted, housewives don't take vows of stability or enclosure, but no cloister ever walled in a soul like three meals a day on a small income.

Penance, *ergo*, is where you find it. What makes it effective is how it is accepted and how much love of God prompts this acceptance. He sent it to us. And that's the best thing about the penance that pops up in lay life. It comes to us, as it were, straight from His hand, fresh and informal. Nowhere is God's transcendent sense of humor more clearly seen. The unexpected little sacrifices He asks of us have a flair proper only to divinity.

Never in a thousand years, for instance, would it have occurred to me to offer up the giant Buddha of Kamakura. That just doesn't cross the average housewife's mind. But one day I did. By a series of most commonplace events, I found myself and four children on shipboard in Yokohama harbor for several hours. Like most of the passengers, we had signed up for a short side trip to Kamakura to see the Buddha, who is forty feet tall and a wonder. I'm told he's really something. I don't know personally, because we never saw him. It had turned out to be Sunday, and we couldn't have the Buddha and Mass too.

At Mass in Yokohama Cathedral we listened instead to a long and apparently eloquent sermon in Japanese, all during which I kept thinking, "We're going to receive Holy Communion with the people we dropped *the* bombs on." When we did receive, the Buddha had diminished considerably in our minds. Still, I feel he'll look nice and rather unusual in our heavenly crowns, topping off all the humdrum candy and chewing gum passed up during Lents.

Incidentally, deciding on your own hook to do without candy and chewing gum—or bread and butter—for forty days can't possibly compare with eating cheerfully for lunch day after day whatever happens to be left in the refrigerator from the night before. In one case you're doing penance, but according to your own will; in the other, you're doing God's, even if the leftovers turn out to be delicious. Being miserable, after all, isn't the reason for mortifying ourselves, though it often makes us so, being what we are.

"Eat," said our Lord, "what is set before you" *(Luke 10:9)*. Who but God would think of setting before you sauerkraut and candied yams? Or a cold hamburger laced with chocolate pudding upset over it? Dishes like that once in a while can give your spiritual life a real boost. That's being really mortified! Anybody can stick to bread and water.

My dictionary tells me, even if St. Paul didn't, that mortify means "to make dead." It comes from two Latin words, naturally: *mors* and *facere*. St. Paul says, "I die daily" *(I Cor. 15:31)*. Our Lord says, "He who loses his life for my sake will find it" *(Matt.*

10:39). Mortification isn't necrosis. Quite the contrary. Even the dictionary makes this plain. It defines it as "to deaden by religious or other discipline, as the carnal affections, bodily appetites, or worldly desires; to abase, to *humble*." (I'll never forget the monk who made me promise to drink a cocktail before dinner for three nights as penance for spiritual pride. He wasn't born yesterday!)

Mortification isn't prayer either. It simply creates a climate for prayer, because when we lose our excessive preoccupation with this world, we become occupied with God and can see Him everywhere. Mortification simply strips us of unessentials.

Our nature isn't bad, but since the Fall it's unruly. Unless we control it by subjecting our wills to God's, we follow it and it runs away with us, like a spirited horse with the bit in its teeth. It's a good horse. The finer the horse, the more likely it is to run. The greatest saints often had the hardest time controlling their human instincts.

St. Paul bemoans the fact that he is "delighted with the law of God according to the inner man, but I see another law in my members, warring against the law of my mind and making me prisoner to the law of sin that is in my members" *(Rom. 7:22-23).*

St. Augustine quoted this passage some 225 times in his writings, so we may presume he had the same trouble as St. Paul and the rest of us. It's with us always. It means we'd rather sleep when the alarm rings, we'd rather knit than do the ironing, we'd rather like to tell off the people on the party line, we'd much rather keep on writing this than get up and go see what that awful ...

XIV. DOING POORLY

Most housewives don't have a lot of money. A fair proportion aspire to wearing mink-dyed muskrat, and some actually achieve real mink. It takes a housewife with real vision, however, to yearn for the peak of Inconspicuous Consumption: muskrat-dyed mink. Not one housewife of my acquaintance owns a muskrat-dyed mink. What abandon this requires! What detachment from worldly opinion in the possession of a solid good! What warmth! What expensive poverty! The spirit faints.

I once got a taste of the kind of exhilaration this could bring on. It happened in a U.S. Commissary in the Orient. For weeks on end we patrons had been supplied with frozen filets mignon from Australia. Monday, Tuesday, Wednesday, every day there was filet mignon, there being no other government-inspected meat to be had.

"Don't you ever cook spaghetti and meat sauce anymore?" asked husband and father.

"I'll see what there is tomorrow," I held out. When I got there, there was filet mignon.

"Give me two pounds please," I said to the boy behind the counter. Then, looking him straight in the eye, "And *grind* it."

"Grind it, mum?"

"GRIND it. Twice, if you please."

He did.

The meat sauce turned out no better than usual, but I think it represents the highest living we've ever done. I never felt so detached from an arbitrary value, existing only in the human mind.

The Curé d'Ars once lighted a fire with a letter containing several hundred francs—on purpose—commenting later on his "expensive ashes." That's what I like about saints. They put the most overworked libertines to shame. They're the only people in the world who ever have any real fun.

85

Robbers locked up in refrigerator cars have been known to burn their stolen greenbacks for a little warmth to stave off freezing to death, learning the relativity of values at the last minute the hard way, but saints know instinctively that no creature of itself can transcend the use to which we put it.

Judas, who was a pedestrian in more ways than one, was simply too sensible to become a saint. He would have saved the price of Mary Magdalene's ointment to give it to the poor. Mary Magdalene, who saw farther than he did, gave it to the poor in one fell swoop by pouring it all at once over our Lord's feet, thereby raising its value exceedingly. She loved much. When people love much, their poverty has all the verve of flaming extravagance. They're known for doing such things as selling everything they have for one little pearl. It's their trademark. Sensible people don't do that.

Poverty in its highest sense, after all, doesn't consist so much in not having anything as in giving away everything one has, constantly. Under normal circumstances, housewives can't take vows of poverty any more than they can take vows of chastity or vows of obedience, but that doesn't exempt them from practicing the virtues of poverty, chastity and obedience. Mary Magdalene was practicing the virtue of poverty when she squandered her ointment.

Thank God for Mary Magdalene! She's a standing reproach to people who take to virtue because they simply don't have enough imagination or enough energy to do anything else. What they practice isn't virtue; it just succeeds in giving virtue a bad name. They bore us to death. Real virtue requires brilliance and abandon. It absorbs every talent one can possibly bring to it.

Poverty is just another instance where the housewife has to shoot for the heights, if she's to shoot for anything at all. She's engaged in the only game in town, and she has to keep doubling the bets to keep playing.

A vow of poverty, be it noted, applies actually only to external possessions. It's good solid muskrat, but only muskrat and good for a start. It's supposed to whet your appetite for mink. Mink in this case being poverty of spirit. When you've achieved that, the only thing left to aspire to is muskrat-dyed mink. This is real poverty which doesn't necessarily look like poverty. It's the kind practiced by holy kings and queens, St. Thomas More, Mary Magdalene, our Lord and His Blessed Mother. None of these was destitute. They owned things, some of them very expensive things, but they were all poor. Many destitute people are far from poor in the gospel sense.

Poverty in lay life is a very tricky virtue to get hold of. Without the help of the Holy Spirit, it's impossible, as our Lord was careful to note. "Like a camel going through the eye of a needle," He said, "but everything is possible with God!" The first step seems obvious: don't acquire anything you don't really need.

On shopping trips with Tina, our littlest "little one," my stock answer to her constant "Oh, Mommy, let's buy that!" has always been, "No, Tina, it's pretty, but we don't need it."

I'll have to think of something else. She's on to me. The last time she picked out some particularly flamboyant and useless gewgaw, she ran to me with it and suggested, "Oh, Mommy, let's *need this!*" What a sermon in five words. (That little child set in our midst is awfully hard to get around!) Is there a human being alive who couldn't persuade himself he needs what he wants? Is there anything that becomes a necessity as quickly as a luxury?

But poverty doesn't automatically eliminate gewgaws, either. That would be too easy, besides making life pretty drab. There are many times in a mother's life when a real spiritual end can be gained much more quickly through a silly piece of costume jewelry than through a new roaster. No hard and fast rules can be drawn. Nor is need any criterion, except as a start. Anybody who can't eventually forgo what he needs isn't really poor.

The perfect practice of poverty brings in its wake all the virtues: humility, patience, purity, truth, justice, liberality, and, ultimately, God. It boils down to what St. John of the Cross calls the way of "*nada*" —ridding oneself progressively of all attachments not leading to God. Beginning with material objects, it opens the path to contemplation, where we forgo even the images in our minds so as to unite more closely with God in prayer. "If thou wilt be perfect," said our Lord to the rich young man, "go, sell what thou hast, and give to the poor" *(Matt. 19:21).*

Spiritually, this is the poverty offered to the housewife. It means purchasing goods without acquiring them. It means being a mother without being a Mom. It expresses itself by almsgiving, freely parting with its substance. It clothes and feeds unfortunates, offers hospitality, bestowing time and work on superiors, equals and inferiors alike. It relinquishes cherished opinions.

It means investing our talents by allowing others the use of them. "Anybody can part with five dollars now and then, but how many can allow others to pick their brains?" said in effect the Little Flower, when a sister in religion palmed off one of the saint's ideas as her own.

This muskrat-dyed mink poverty is very hard to practice. Like being mortified in a simple way, it doesn't show much. It can be awfully spiritual. It often goes so far as doing without Mass, spiritual direction, frequently the Sacraments. It means giving away to others poorer than ourselves indulgences and satisfactions for good works. It means doing without the supports and privileges of the religious state. Poverty means being content to appear even less good than one is, grinding filet mignon into hamburger any old time. It copes humbly with the inconvenience of possessions, as well as limitations of income.

Ah, income. Let's not sneer at the more common, more material forms of poverty! Income is a creative limitation in the housewife's life which can whittle a volume of dull prose into a sparkling sonnet. It operates on all economic levels, exercising an unseen but potent influence on the décor of her home, the scope of her sins, the kind of dessert on the table, her hair style, sense of humor, right down to the quality of her Missal. It defines her rule, directs untold details of her earthly existence and molds her virtues. God wills it.

He certainly wills that most incomes are never large enough to allow us to do all we please. This is a great blessing to the housewife. It keeps her minding her own business more than she would ordinarily, often eliminating the servant problem by eliminating the servants. That makes a certain amount of manual labor necessary, thereby keeping her figure within bounds and opening treasures of prayer and humility. It perfects hope. It keeps her dependent on her husband, God's immediate representative for her. It forces her to bring up her children in habits of thrift and industry, teaching them to turn out lights and not tear their buttons off.

It develops prudence and keeps her from insulting her husband's boss, as she might well do if she ever came into any real money. It eradicates hosts of unessentials which might hinder her on her way to God, and generally keeps her out of expensive mischief. Gambling and divorce, for instance. The benefits are endless. The mistakes a housewife avoids through lack of cash are just so many marvels of God's prevenient grace.

One of its best effects is that it keeps her from looking forward to being canonized. On All Saints' Day, Holy Mother Church sings out St. John's vision of heaven, saying, "I saw a great multitude which no man could number, out of all nations ... standing before the throne" *(Apoc. 7:9).*

These are the vulgar in glory, and you can bet an awful lot of them are housewives. They've finally reached the City where there's no sun to sun, the Lamb being the lamp thereof, and woman's work is finally done. Just who they are, however, won't be known until we get there ourselves to find out. The truth is, a canonization takes a lot of money, and any housewife can practice real spiritual poverty right off by forgetting about it.

Now, never let it be said it requires money to become a saint. Canonization itself adds nothing to a saint's sanctity, for it is simply the official recognition of a transformation already accomplished by Almighty God. Saints are canonized not for God, or for themselves, but for us. They are presented to us as examples of particular virtues or ways of life for our emulation and in order that we may ask them personally to help us. Saints appear at particular times for particular purposes. Multiplying canonizations indiscriminately would serve no purpose.

And canonizations are expensive. They require exhaustive research into the life of the prospective candidate, costly inquiry into depositions of hundreds of witnesses, over a period of years. It therefore takes a national movement, extraordinary popular interest, a well-established religious order, or all three to foot the bill. A private family could hardly get its sainted aunt beatified unless her sphere of influence had been unusually broad. I've heard of a wealthy layman who tried to beat this limitation by leaving a large bequest in his will to cover his own canonization costs, but, well, you can see where that leads.

Anyway we know that the vast majority of saints, probably some of the greatest, are never canonized, having been created for purposes known only to God. It is to this segment of the heavenly population that the housewife, through her poverty, may be invited.

For her, forgetting about getting canonized may be the first degree of real humility, without which the whole operation is impossible. We might just remember, too, that our Lady became the mother of the Messias only after she had apparently renounced all hope of it by taking a vow of virginity, and that Abraham, destined to have descendants as many as the stars of heaven, was ordered to sacrifice his only son. Poverty and faith sometimes get so close as to be almost indistinguishable in practice.

I used to try to stretch our income by keeping a household account book. I could say it got my goat, but the truth is, my goat got it. He ate it.

I remember it was a sunny day in spring. I was standing on the front porch holding the book and a pencil behind me, leaning over the rail. Calling to my husband, who was out in the field, "Gustav, how much did you say you paid for the—!" I felt a gentle tug. On turning, I saw Gregory the goat, who had just broken loose again from his tether under the locusts. (Anchor chain wouldn't hold him.) He had snuck up on the porch with his customary agility, and had soon smelled PAPER, which he loved with the love of an historical novelist. Whenever we had candy bars on the lawn, we would eat the candy, and he would eat the wrappers, making for exemplary tidiness all around. He was now ingesting a large chunk he had just bitten out of the notebook, metal spirals and all, with no more trouble than if it had been our best rosebush. (He ate rosebushes when he couldn't get thistles or paper.)

"Paid for WHAT?" yelled Gustav, still far afield.

"NEVER mind!" I shouted back. "Here," I said to the beast, "you might as well make a meal of it," and I gave him the rest of our accounts. He ate them up, additions, subtractions, errors and all, betraying nothing like the pain they had caused me.

I've never kept accounts since. I don't mean we don't budget. We just don't keep accounts. There's all the difference.

That was a real liberation, not given to everyone in this vale of tears, and we're no less solvent than before. I'm not against keeping accounts as such, but I know it has nothing to do with being rich or poor. Lots of rich people keep accounts, and lots of poor people keep accounts, without ever getting poorer or richer.

Judas kept accounts. If he were among us today—and he is—it's just possible he might tot up his indulgences every Saturday night. I can see the columns now: plenaries in the hundreds column, years in the tens, days in the units. Special entries for novenas, First Fridays, and visits to the sick.

When she appeared before God, said the Little Flower, she would take good care to be empty-handed. She made plenty of novenas and only God knows how many indulgences she gained for you and me, but she didn't carry them around with her.

"For the rich He has sent empty away" *(Luke 1:53)*, said our Lady, who gave away God.

XV. STEPHEN

I've confessed children baffle me. Now, one of my favorite Catholics is a child. This is partly due to his being our son Stephen, but I think it's mostly due to his being five years old. A lot of my favorite Catholics are five years old.

This one is quite toothless in the upper front, having lost three teeth on a terrazzo floor at the age of three, and at present writing has no imminent hope of the second set. He has a way of gazing off into the distance with his mouth open, and his general aspect is that of the abandoned orphan aspiring to a college education. This gets him everything he wants.

His favorite game is pretending to be a monkey, and he can look alarmingly like one when he pleases. On his first visit to the monastery over our mountain "to see the monks," he was plainly disappointed. It was monkeys he had had in mind. The men in the black and white habits were not his only surprise. Looking about the monastery chapel, beautiful and austere like the Order—from which simpering pink art is happily and conspicuously absent —he whispered worriedly, "Muvver, are you sure this is a *Caflick* church?" When I assured him it was, he seemed quite pleased. He knelt to say his Hail Mary. I knelt to thank God for separating Himself from pastel plaster in Stephen's mind.

Stephen is full of unutterable wisdom. Wordsworth would have doted on him, in theory. In the middle of a snowstorm some time back, he announced, putting on his coat, "I'm going out to pick some flowers."

We, being adult and of lesser faith, quite naturally remarked there wouldn't be any. Why not stay in and play a game?

"Oh, I'll find some." And out he went.

In ten minutes he was back with a drooping hollyhock leaf, very brown around the edges, and a piece of periwinkle stem, still green and probably pried out from under a rock in the rock garden.

Without a word to us, he went to his favorite treasure trove, the kitchen trash box. (We have a terrible time throwing anything away at our house. Every item comes back into circulation at least once.) He found a suitable small bottle, filled it with water, and arranged the "flowers."

"I'm going to give this to Baby. She doesn't have anything to look at," says he.

When we went upstairs later, there it was, the whole arrangement placed in the center of a chair in full view of the crib. Baby of course understood the matter perfectly and gazed at the marvel wonderingly for as long as her powers of concentration permitted. We couldn't help looking at it ourselves. Definitely, it had something—like the thighbone of a saint, to dust returning, but full of nagging invitation into unfathomable mystery.

Stephen had been praying for snow some weeks before this particular snowstorm began. The first flakes fell on December 26, which just happens to be the Feast of Stephen. That morning, the family exclaimed:

"Look, Stephen, your snow!"

"Yes, I know," he said, watching the flakes come down, "that's because it's the Feast of ME."

Then he went on eating his oatmeal, wiggling as usual in his chair, swinging his legs, poking one of his brothers surreptitiously with his elbow, hoping to stir up a little excitement.

"Let's go up in the attic and play trains," he said, as the last of the cereal disappeared. "After chores," he added, catching my eye. The snow, obviously, could wait.

And He took a little child and set him in their midst, not just once, two thousand years ago, but millions of times, in all the homes of the world. "For of such," He told us, "is the kingdom of heaven." The only thing He made more of than housewives is little children. Little children are very, very vulgar.

"Who made you, Stephen?"

"God made me. Can I have a banana?"

Inasmuch as God also made the banana, and this particular banana because Stephen was destined to ask for it, only spiritual schizophrenics would find fault with that answer.

When Lent last rolled around, all the children got together and made a few public announcements about what they were "giving up." There's nothing like a public announcement to make you stick to a resolution, though we like to point out it's the ones you keep to yourself that do the most good. When I say all the children, however, I mean all the children except Stephen. He didn't say anything.

"Stephen, aren't you giving up anything?"

"Oh, I'm giving up my *sins*," he answered wearily. No use in further discussion. No use particularizing. At five, the contemplative, all-of-a-piece approach comes quite naturally.

"Why don't you make your bed up straight!" said his brother, three years older. When this lad was five, he was rather "contemplative" too, but after television, a couple of brushes with the school bully, and the worries of a limited allowance, he sees the forest is full of trees and the world is multiplicity. He has already started out on that long ascetical climb our Lord labeled "except ye *become* as little children."

But Stephen hasn't left his Father's house yet. Only this morning he was intoning on a plastic ukulele (in a roughly Lydian mode):

> Oh, I was a farmer
> With a hat on my head,
> The reins in my hand
> And the saddle on the cow ...

Plunk, strum.

> High-ho, high-ho,
> And the bunglebees
> Were fast asleeeeeeeeeep.

Plunk, strum, strum, continued Stephen. He's a country boy.

He knows cows never wear saddles. But then it's the adult world that's so full of curious consistencies.

"*Dominus vobiscum,*" he chants most any old time, rummaging in the toy box.

Like his Church, he is quite universal. No one has told him Latin is too hard to learn, so he has no trouble with it. Baby sings the best Gregorian in the family. Both will have to be much older before they can espouse such provincialisms as the "vernacular movement." I promise Stephen won't hear about it from me, but it's bound to happen soon.

The day before he sang the song, he asked very seriously, "How come God was born on Christmas?" This kind of question is the beginning of adulthood. It's the sort of question modern philosophers ask.

"How can there be a God when man's will is free?" ask atheist existentialists.

Tell Stephen God made Christmas Christmas, and all will become clear to him. Tell an existentialist that man's will is free because God made it free, and he will smile at you indulgently ... especially if you're a housewife, set in the midst of little children.

He needs so badly to get back to the bunglebees.

And I'd better get back to my ironing, because after that I've got a catechism lesson to prepare. For little children, you have to be prepared—not that it does much good.

XVI. MOUTHS OF BABES

"Go to hell!" yelled a dozen determined, high-pitched little voices from across the hall. Horrible, but unmistakable.

"They've mutinied," was my first thought. The primary class had mutinied. I wondered if I should go rescue my fellow catechist, whom I imagined pinned helpless on the rectory sofa like Gulliver among the Lilliputians. (She teaches in the parlor; I get the older children in the dining room.) Luckily the terrible anathema stopped before I dashed out and made a fool of myself. I learned later that the little innocents were merely answering a routine, though all-important question.

"Now, what happens to souls that die in mortal sin?" asked their teacher. "They ..."

Seems everybody knew the answer to that one. Naturally they weren't going to pass up an opportunity like that to say a bad word and get commended for it to boot.

Professional catechists no doubt take such little incidents in stride and hardly notice, but as I keep reminding you, I'm a housewife. There are 20,000 souls in our parish. Of these some 432 are Catholics, and about half of them are children. No nuns. No parochial school. Just these little bits of leaven in a great, big lumpy loaf. This means catechism is even more important here than it might be in most places, and it's up to us. It gets taught after school by Father and as many (guess who?) housewives as he can talk into it by judicious application of spiritual thumbscrews.

I'm one of them. I've got the third and fourth grades, and I spend my time in class falling in and out of traps of my own setting. The children may learn a little from me, but I learn plenty from them.

My sanctification is in no way hindered, because in class or out I'm driven to spend more time praying for help than teaching or correcting papers. It's no surprise to me that special guidance and

96

protection are begged for catechists in the Mass itself. At the prayer *Te Igitur* which occurs at the beginning of the Canon, when the congregation prays for the Pope, its Bishop, and its clergy, we also pray for a group designated as "*apostolicae fidei cultoribus*" —cultivators of the apostolic faith.

The word *cultor* is hard to translate into just one English word. Actually it means "planter" or "laborer" and would apply to parents as well as teachers. Ideally, it includes all believers, all workers in the Lord's vineyard. To me, on Friday afternoons at 3:30 when my class meets, *cultor* means "catechist," and I take great comfort in the thought that all over the world, in all Masses in all churches, the faithful habitually pray for me.

When the Little Flower was assigned the direction of the novices in her convent—an advanced form of catechism involving total spiritual formation—she liked to think of herself as a little dish set out for kittens to feed from. Because she was a saint, she never doubted the *bon Jésus* would fill the dish at the appointed times with whatever was necessary for the supernatural education of her charges. Especially, said she, if the little dish were careful to stay on the ground.

"On the ground" means radical humility. For anybody who tries to tell children about God, it's the only safe position. Moving from it is pure madness, let alone a lapse in virtue.

I often think of the Jewish doctors questioning the boy Jesus in the Temple, of how "all who were listening to him were amazed at his understanding and his answers" *(Luke 2:47)*. My sympathies are with those doctors. This joyful mystery, it seems to me, is the catechist's mystery par excellence, because through the attitude of the teachers in the Temple the Holy Spirit holds before us a luminous truth: Those whom we are empowered to instruct will inevitably instruct us.

This instruction can take surprising turns.

"Who was the only human being ever born without original sin?" I asked the class once.

"Mary!" they shouted.

"That's right. Now, what is the special name we call her that means she was born sinless?"

Dead silence. Then one small hand goes up. "Yes?" I prod.

"We call her the Immaculate Contraception!"

Many books can be filled by the outrageous sayings of children. Any teacher, any mother, could supply at least one volume. I'm bringing this one up not to fill this chapter, certainly not to be funny, but to drive you and all the rest of the *fidei cultores* to our knees.

The little girl who gave this reply couldn't have been more innocent. She had big, wide-open eyes and honest enthusiasm, and she was happy at being able to give an answer. But she lives in the world with us, and that world seeps into the cracks of every Christian home. It hangs heavy even over the nursery.

What to say to my little apostle living in our sea of unbelievers? Nothing. To her the word contraception means the beginning of life, not murder. I corrected her, but her pronunciation only. Her answer, in her child's heart, was absolutely correct.

As for the coiners of the word she used, our Lord has already promised them a terrible reward. "Whoever causes one of these little ones who believe in me to sin, it were better for him to have a great millstone hung around his neck, and to be drowned in the depths of the sea" *(Matt. 17:6)*.

Another time, we got on the subject of "offering it up." "What are some of the things we can offer up?"

"I fell down the steps this morning."

"I got spanked."

"My brother tore my shirt, and I kicked him!" (I have a sneaking suspicion God loves children because, among other virtues, they don't fake virtue where they haven't got it.)

"I had a sore throat last week. Maybe I'll have to have my tonsils out."

"The cat scratched me."

"Well," I said, "those are all good things to offer up, but is that the only kind of suffering there is, the kind that hurts your body?"

"Oh, no!" they all said at once, with terrible conviction. "Well, name some other kinds," I suggested.

The room became strangely quiet, because suddenly all of us were thinking. We were thinking about those other kinds of suffering. I should have known better than to ask such a question.

I had meant, give me some hypothetical cases, but children aren't hypothetical. They are realists who delight in the concrete. It's only adults who hide behind "I know somebody who."

Before I could forestall what I knew would be poignant soul-baring, it came.

A chubby little girl said quietly and sincerely, without bothering to raise her hand, "At school they call me Fatso."

She relapsed into silence, and nobody said anything. Especially not I. It was hard to go on, because suddenly the monstrous, suppurating scandal of the universe lay exposed before us: the hidden suffering of little children. Caryll Houselander has called this pain the Passion of the Infant Christ, because He too endured it. He sanctified it for all time, and He continues to redeem the world with it.

Who can deny the torment of ridicule? Our Lord endured it all His life, and it was one of the more refined tortures of His Passion. "He saved others, Himself He cannot save!" *(Matt. 27:42)*, He was taunted with on the cross. Pilate's soldiers called Him—not Fatso, to be sure—but King of the Jews, with a scorn possible only to proud ignorance. When He stood bleeding in the wounds of the Roman scourging, "They stripped Him and put on Him a scarlet cloak; and plaiting a crown of thorns, they put it upon His head, and a reed into His right hand, and bending the knee before Him, they mocked Him" *(Matt. 27:28-29)*.

By submitting to that gruesome burlesque in the Procurator's courtyard, the Word made flesh transformed ridicule into an instrument of God's mercy. Even my little Fatso's qualifies. It has become the treasure of saints, yet it is lavishly accorded to all of us. In a way, however, it remains the special pain of little children. Not only are they defenseless against it, being as yet free of the rationalizations adults devise to deflect it, but they mercilessly inflict it on one another, heedlessly and quite effortlessly.

It is only when one has been ridiculed enough oneself that one truly ceases ridiculing others. This is why, again, we are commanded, not to remain little children, but to become little children, to learn compassion through suffering.

Children aren't sentimental, so let's not sentimentalize about them. They can be cruel. They possess the Faith whole and entire, much like their father Abraham. It's all there, but it's not developed. Nowhere can this be seen better than in their ideas about prayer. Mind, I didn't say their prayer, I said their ideas about prayer. They pray very well.

"Can you pray without asking God for something?" "No!" they assured me.

"No?" So I read them part of the Eighth Psalm.

> Oh Lord, our Lord,
> how glorious is your name over all the earth!
> You have exalted your majesty above the heavens.
> Out of the mouths of babes and sucklings
> you have fashioned praise because of your foes,
> to silence the hostile and the vengeful.
> When I behold your heavens, the work of your fingers,
> the moon and the stars which you set in place—
> What is man that you should be mindful of him,
> or the son of man that you should care for him?

"Is that a prayer?"

Puzzlement all around the dining room table. I tried to explain that it was, but I felt they weren't really convinced. Why is it that prayer, to children and childish adults, must be synonymous with "gimme"? Is this the fault of our civilization, of our Catholic instruction, or is the prayer of praise something which is not instinctual, but must be the result of spiritual maturity? I don't know.

Certainly a child of school age doesn't praise God as a cat or a mountain praises Him, simply by existing according to its nature. His prayer must be immanent, but also articulate, willed.

Who can explain the prayer of praise to a child? Yet this prayer is above all the child's prayer. It is the prayer we pray well only when we have become little children.

On Palm Sunday, as we read in St. Matthew's account of the Passion *(Matt. 21:15-16)*, it was "the children crying out in the temple and saying, 'Hosanna to the Son of David!'" which had so angered the chief priests and the Scribes.

Jesus, coming to their defense as He always does, said, "Have you never read, 'Out of the mouths of babes and sucklings you have fashioned praise'?"

We can be sure the children shouted even louder after this, as children do when they find somebody to take up for them. "Hosanna to the Son of David! Blessed is He who comes in the name of the Lord! Hosanna in the highest!"

This most beautiful praise of the Messias has become one of our most familiar prayers. It is set like a bright jewel in the very midst of the Mass the Messias came to institute, and occurs just before the prayer for catechists. It is coupled dramatically with the thunder of the Seraphim before the throne of God, overheard by the prophet Isaias in a vision.

"SANCTUS! SANCTUS! SANCTUS!" the great spirits cry to one another, veiling God's majesty with their wings.

"HOSANNA IN THE HIGHEST!" pipe the children right after them, rushing in as children always do, where angels fear to tread.

"Blessed is He who comes in the name of the Lord! Hosanna in the highest!" squeak all the catechism classes.

Now, how am I going to get all this across to them as well as they got it across to me?

XVII. THE CHILDREN'S ROOM

Every once in a while my husband and I engage in "pedal-car praying." This means we're asking for some fantastically big grace which we have no right whatever to expect, but which we have every hope of getting just the same. As might be suspected, we got the idea from Stephen, and it happened in this way:

About a month before Christmas, when we asked him what he wanted, he said, "I want a tractor-trike." He was praying for it. The one he wanted was expensive and more than his usual allocation, but of course he had us on the spot. We ended by getting it and hid it among the garden chairs in the springhouse loft. Three days before Christmas his uncle arrived with a blue pedal-car with very few dents in it, which the older cousins had outgrown.

"Thought you might like to give this to Stephen," he said.

"He must be about the right size for it by now."

Stephen was the right size. But, well ... it would be nice. If we had only known ... we had already bought the tractor ... two presents like that were really too much at one time ... for one child. What's worse the other children would have to be faced.

"Thanks," we said. "We'll take it."

We put it in the springhouse, vaguely meaning to save it for a later occasion. Naturally, on Christmas Day, which comes only once a year, we gave it to Stephen along with the tractor. Nobody minded.

He accepted both with joy and gladness, but a really unnerving complacency. We wondered. Had he managed to stumble across it in the loft?

"Stephen, aren't you awfully surprised to get the car?"

"Oh, no," he said. "I was praying for that too."

St. Jeanne de Chantal always set children to praying when she wanted something very badly, her own children or anybody else's. Obviously, if you've got access to atomic power, you're a fool not to use it.

102

"Pray, Stephen," I said the last time I was caught in a howling blizzard miles from home with him and his baby sister in a stalled station wagon. Stephen closed his eyes, put his nose in the air and opened his mouth, and two angels disguised as mechanics drove up in a truck.

"Help you, lady?" they asked.

"See?" said Tavy, when his father entered the Church and was baptized on a February 29th. "I asked for that at my First Communion!"

Certainly children's power over the heart of God is known to all nuns who have anything to do with them. I often wonder how statistics run on school picnics and May Days saved from certain rain by nuns setting children to praying. I have a friend who is a nun in the jungles of Assam. Her work consists in picking up children nobody wants (mostly girls) and bringing them to God.

"Don't worry," she sometimes writes me. "Have faith. I'll ask Julia to pray for you," as if that settled the matter, any matter. Julia is the ace up Mother's ample sleeve. She is a little feeble-minded Indian girl who will probably never be able to make her own living in this world, but who knows God quite well and has probably developed her intellect to nearer its full capacity than you or I have.

After the pedal-car incident I seriously thought of taking Stephen aside and trying to switch him off the "prayer of gimme" to "something more spiritual." Considering his fondness for monkeys and the Divine Irony, I'm not sure I could take a live orangutan in stride come. next Christmas, should one be discovered in the springhouse. I say I thought about it, but I didn't dare. Frankly, children's prayer is something I wouldn't dream of tampering with. I'd rather cope with the monkey, which is something I understand better.

On our bookshelves, I've just counted twenty-six books dealing with prayer, most of them purchased by me. This offers proof positive that I don't know anything about it, but also that I'm dying to find out. So far all I've managed to learn from them is that the more "advanced" you become, the more you pray the way Stephen prays right now. (As the young Indian said, "What do you mean, work hard so I can retire and do nothing? I'm doing nothing right now!")

When you pray like Stephen you don't use many words, because he doesn't know many. Julia, I guess, knows even less. You also ask for outrageous things, such as a tractor AND a pedal-car for Christmas, without being embarrassed about it, or the conversion of the whole world, or being swallowed up whole in the Will of God, dragging everybody else with you, all at once. Like the Little Flower, you'll take the whole doggone workbasket, thank you.

All saints pray this way. St. Teresa, who wrote a sublime treatise on the Our Father, said that you don't insult a great prince disposed to give you a kingdom by asking him for pins and needles! She didn't understand people who from false modesty aspired to Purgatory and "a little place just inside the pearly gates."

If I understand the matter rightly, this sort of thing is being a "mystic." A mystic, as nearly as I can figure, is anybody who can go straight to an object and call a spade a spade. Mystics don't write long letters or postcards to somebody who's right in the same room with them, as God is. They write letters if they're made to, but they think it's pretty silly. Mystics can't wait to be saints to pray, either. "Take good, gracious God as He is, plat and plain as a plaster, and lay it to thy sick self as thou art," says the Epistle of Privy Council with typical mystical vulgarity.

"But the Emperor has no clothes!" said a little mystic once, and everybody tried to hush him up.

When Tavy was Stephen's age, he had a little Filipino friend called Facundo. Facundo came to the door one day and said something that sounded like, "Gobbledy gobbledy sa maganda gook gong?" or something equally unintelligible, to Tavy.

"Well, wait a minute, Facundo," said Tavy, "and I'll see if mother will let me out."

"Why, Tavy," I said, "I didn't know you could understand Tagalog."

"I can't," said Tavy. "That's just what Facundo says when he wants me to bring my toys over."

That's being mystical, I think. Children are all that way until they learn to be otherwise and have to wade through twenty-six books to get back where they started. Mysticism isn't just a way of praying. It's an attitude toward life.

Prayer can't be described. It is. Like St. Benedict and anyone else who knows how to pray well, our Lord says very little about it. He said simply, "When you pray," and went on from there. It's true He set an example to us by spending long nights "in the prayer of God," praying in the desert, at His baptism and the Transfiguration, on mountain tops and in Gethsemane. He recited the Psalms and engaged obediently in all the public worship which was the duty of the pious Israelite. The night before He died, He gave us the text of His prayer to His Father, asking that we might all be one.

About prayer in common He said merely that it was very efficacious: "If two of you shall agree on earth about anything at all for which they ask, it shall be done for them by my Father in heaven" *(Matt. 18:19)*.

Children, being wise enough to know no better, hear this and act on it. A few months back Stephen and Tavy got together and prayed for a *real* tractor. We didn't know about it until last Saturday, when my husband came home with one from a country auction.

"It was such a bargain," was about all he could find to tell me, looking fairly foolish. Though we live in the country, he isn't a farmer. He commutes to work.

Stephen, who was in the know, said, "Tavy's been praying for it every night!" and jumped for joy. "Can I ride it, Daddy? Can I? Now?" Evidently, for something that size, he felt you have to have help. Coincidence?

But that's the trouble with children. They pray just the way our Lord instructed us to pray. "Don't use many words, as the Gentiles do," He said.

"Could we please have a tractor?" asked Tavy and Stephen. When Gedeon set out to conquer the Madianites, God told him he'd never accomplish his purpose with 32,000 soldiers. "You have too many soldiers," the Almighty told him bluntly. "Lest

Israel vaunt itself against me and say, 'My own power brought me the victory'" *(Judges 7:2-3)*. This is a lesson in prayer.

"'Lead them down to the water,'" God commanded Gedeon.

> "You shall set to one side everyone who laps up the water as a dog does with its tongue; to the other, everyone who kneels down to drink." Those who lapped up the water raised to their mouths by hand numbered three hundred. ... The Lord said to Gedeon, "By means of the three hundred who lapped up the water I will save you and will deliver Madian into your power. So let all the other soldiers go home." *(Judges 7:4-7)*

Mystics and children lap, because it's quicker to drink that way. Madianites don't catch them off their feet in a vulnerable position.

"Don't use many words, as the Gentiles do," He said. Our Lord would have been the last person in the world to push a pamphlet full of aspirations under your nose to memorize by Tuesday. Many words are impossible for people who pray all the time, as we are commanded. The Gospel hints, however, that the disciples might have liked our Lord to give a lengthy discourse on prayer. They asked Him—it might have been in the last year of His ministry—to teach them to pray. They actually seemed a little annoyed with Him. He was so hard to pin down when it came to anything specific about prayer. "John the Baptist taught *his* disciples to pray," they said in effect, "why don't you teach us?"

In answer to their prodding, He taught them the Lord's Prayer. As St. Luke reports it, however, it was almost as if He had said, "Well, if you must use particular words in your private prayers, use these," or, "pray along these lines." Then He told them to call God Father, as small children do. He told them to ask for necessities ("Give us this day our daily bread"), and great, cosmic graces like "Thy kingdom come, Thy will be done, on earth as it is in heaven" *(Luke 10:2-3)*, a really scandalous request!

Then, of course, our Lord taught us to nag our Father, as children do, into giving us what we desire. He devoted two parables to illustrate this point. One was about a man who woke up his friend in the middle of the night to get some bread for an unexpected visitor. "I say to you, although he will not get rip and give to him because he is his friend, yet because of his persistence he will get up and give him all he needs" *(Luke 11:8-9).*

"Mother, fix my string."

"Not now, Stephen, can't you see I'm up to my ears in paint?"

"But it's got knots!" "Not now, Stephen!"

"But I can't fix my truck without the string." He stands there about one minute, his eye never leaving the course of the paint brush.

"Can you fix it now?"

Maybe you have strong nerves, and can continue painting with two little beady eyes watching for the slightest indecisive move toward the paint can. I can't. I fix the string.

"Can I have a cookie?" he asks, as I struggle with the knots. No point in just standing there waiting, he figures.

"Yes!" If even God gives in, how can I hope to withstand?

"Therefore, if you, evil as you are," said eternal Wisdom, "know how to give good things to your children, how much more will your Father in Heaven give the good things to those who ask Him!" *(Matt. 7:11).*

He did say, however, to be unobtrusive about it. "When you pray, go into thy room, and closing thy door, pray to thy Father in secret; and thy Father, who sees in secret, will reward thee" *(Matt. 6:6).* The children's room, as every mother knows, is any room they happen to be in.

Children, I think, are mystics, and we're commanded to become like them.

XVIII. MISSIONARIES IN THE PARLOR

Children are scavengers, too. Everything they pick up is brought home and eventually dropped in the living room. Some years back, in Manila, I found a German missionary left sitting on the sofa. He had a mild nervous tremor, and I was happy to learn later that he had acquired it before meeting up with us.

The children had attracted him by waving to him every day at one o'clock as he passed by their school on a motorbike, his white cassock skirts flying, on his way to a class in accounting at Santo Tomas University. I don't know what story they gave him, but they succeeded in getting him home with them, no doubt angling for a ride on the bike. Luckily, he loved children.

Conversation was difficult at first, because "Fader's" English was embryonic, but it got better as he continued to visit us. It wasn't long before we asked him that question the laity for some reason seem compelled to ask any priest they feel they know well enough.

"How can you stand hearing confessions? Don't they make you feel *slimy*?"

"Zlimy?" Fader's vocabulary hadn't reached this far. "Dirty."

"Ach, no!" replied Fader. "Convessions I like most!" We stared a little, I guess.

"No, no. Ven I come here to Philippines, I esk my superior to gif me very many convessions to hear. Ah, if you know how der people suffer! Zo much suffering! Und only in der convessional sometimes dey tell. Zo much suffering nobody effer know ... iss zo goot to gif dem liddle conzolation. Der *vomen*, especial. Iss zo hidden. Nobody vould belief!"

With that burst, probably the longest he had ever delivered in English, he gazed out the window and lapsed into silence. So did I, for once. It isn't often a man takes female suffering that seriously, and well, it confused me.

It shouldn't have. We learned later that there was a good reason for Fader's little nervous tremor. He had only recently been released from a Chinese Communist prison. After three years of the mental and physical torture of the kind the rest of us read about in the papers, he could smell suffering in others like a rat terrier smells rats. He told us all about it eventually, very simply and matter-of-factly, piece by piece, in the same tone he used to tell us about his struggles with accounting. Every time I think of "Fader," I feel guilty about the cushions on our chairs and the roast in the refrigerator.

He's still in the Philippines, in a remote northern province where he eats rice three times a day, struggling with dialects and dysentery, possessing nothing but his three vows and shepherding a little brown-skinned flock to whom he teaches catechism.

"The people here are very poor, but so good and kind. I am very well," he told us in his last letter, his English much improved.

I don't mean to say a priest must undergo three years of Communist torture to appreciate a housewife's sufferings, but it helps. Nasty as suffering is, there's no shorter cut to compassion. God Himself made use of it. St. Paul says of our Lord "For in that He Himself has suffered and has been tempted, He is able to help those who are tempted" *(Heb. 2:18)*.

I had personal experience of this in a small way while I was trying out the "simple mortification, my child" of going without water. I found myself positively obsessed with fetching cold water for anybody who so much as looked in my direction. Everybody, it seemed to me, was unaccountably thirsty.

I offered some once to a Jehovah's Witness. She was canvassing our neighborhood during the hottest part of the siesta and appeared damp with perspiration at our door, weighed down by a monstrous heavy black bookbag.

"Are you the lady of the house?" she asked. "I'll get you a drink," I said. "Come in."

She must have been rather surprised, but in she came, and bottomed up without being pressed further. (Actually I gave her not water, but fruit juice, so I could have some with her and make it a social occasion. Don't worry. I weaseled plenty.)

"May I ask your name?" she queried politely, in her almost but-not-quite English accent.

I told her.

She nodded, looked at my nose, and without preamble dived into the black bag, extracting a large volume. "Will you allow me to read to you from your Bible? You *are* Jewish, aren't you?"

I had to admit I wasn't, after fighting down the urge to masquerade, just to see what would happen. "But I wish I were," I added. "Jews make the very best Catholics."

"Oh." She put it very quietly and shortly. Then, "You are a *Catholic*?" There was some reason for her surprise, because outside religious, there are relatively few American Catholics in the Philippines.

"Yes, I am," I said staunchly. It was something of a profession of faith, because from the look in her pretty eyes, I half expected to see her reach into the black bag again, pull out a gun and shoot me dead between the eyes with a "Take that, you whore of Babylon!"

As a matter of fact, she did reach into the bag, but thank goodness, only to pullout another volume.

"This," she said very clearly and distinctly, emphasizing each word, "is a Catholic Bible." She allowed a few moments for the import of her words to sink in, because obviously she believed this was the first time in my life I had ever been allowed to see one so close. "Will you allow me to read to you from it?"

"Sure," I said. "Why not?"

She opened it and began reading carefully as one reads to a small child the passage in St. Luke where our Lord teaches His disciples the Lord's Prayer. I was quite touched. She was bringing me the Good News. In all this torrid heat!

But, of course, she had walked into the spider's parlor. To make a long story short, we were soon at it hammer and tongs. Quotations flew back and forth, Catholic version, Protestant version, Witness version, until both of us practically in the same breath mentioned the fact that the Devil didn't mind quoting Scripture when it suited his purpose. She meant me, and I meant her.

We got along fine after that. I learned she was Welsh, and had never been out of Wales until she and her husband went to the United States to train for evangelizing the Philippines. They were here to wrest the Islands from the grasp of the Roman Anti-Christ who labors to keep the inhabitants as ignorant as possible. My guest worked one side of the street while her husband worked the other.

I also learned that before this trip, she had never had any direct contact with so much as one Catholic, her first exposure being to six priests who happened to come over on the same freighter with her. One, she admitted under pressure, "was probably one of the kindest men I have ever known." This priest was "Fader." His was the only name she remembered.

What a coincidence! About as much a coincidence as having five fingers on each hand. When the Holy Spirit tosses you the ball, you jolly well have to do something with it, not just stand there. But what?

Guileless as the serpent, I decided to let her show me the errors of my ways. "You know, my religion obliges me to search for the truth," I commented jesuitically.

After a half-hour of instructing me, she was amazed to learn that Catholics don't believe only professed Catholics go to heaven.

"Are you sure?" she asked. "I've never heard that!"

"Oh, absolutely," I said. Then I threw in invincible ignorance, the visible and invisible Church, a short discourse on actual grace, Msgr. Knox, and wound up with the obligation to follow conscience according to St. Thomas—all under the general heading of "Catholics aren't nearly as stupid as they can look."

"You know," she said, "I think you really believe!"

"Of course I really believe!" I was really warmed up by then.

"All Catholics really believe!"

"Oh, no they don't," she informed me. "All I've ever met up with here is credulity, not faith!"

I tried to explain to her that Filipinos had been critically short of priests for half a century, that many might be uninstructed, but that didn't mean they didn't possess the Faith.

"You just talk to Catholics who can't always express themselves, maybe," I ventured. Poor young lady, she had just walked into one who had, if not the gift of tongues, at least the gift of gab! She wasn't convinced, she said. But she gave me credit for misguided sincerity, and then looked at her watch.

"I've got to be on my way. My husband's going to wonder what happened to me." With that she got up.

"Well," I twitted, "if you really expect to convert any of us, you'll at least have to learn more about what we're supposed to believe. Wait a minute. I'll be right back."

I dashed into the bedroom and quickly scanned our meager apologetical library. "Veni, Creator," I breathed, and landed on a paperback copy of Karl Adam's *Spirit of Catholicism*.

"Here," I said, proffering it about as nonchalantly as I would a hamburger with a worm pill in it, "take this for your mission library. It'll be a useful reference."

"Why, thank you," she said, the pamphleteer pamphleteered, "I'll read it. I really will." She dropped the Truth into the satchel with all the other Truths and half-truths.

"And drop in again anytime you're in the neighborhood." She couldn't do that. "We have to leave next Monday for Cebu. One of our missionaries just died there and we have to replace him."

When we got to the door, she paused. "Thanks for the drink, too." Then, "Would you accept something from me?"

"With pleasure," I said.

She handed me two large pamphlets. When she had gone, I looked into them. They were all about the coming earthly kingdom and lions lying down with lambs, and immortality not being for just everybody. Only 144,000 can make it to the celestial kingdom, they announced.

I would have burst into tears, if I could have spared the moisture. She was working so hard, and she was so thirsty. I've never known anybody thirstier, except the Christ whose divinity she denies.

"I thirst," He said from the cross, very plainly. And, "Give me a drink," He once asked a Samaritan woman.

A year or so later I read in a Catholic magazine that we shouldn't have anything to do with Jehovah's Witnesses. They should be ignored. Gosh, honest, I didn't know. Apparently Fader didn't either. When I told him about my visitor, he didn't seem particularly surprised. He promised to remember her at Mass, because I don't think he believes in coincidences either.

You please pray for her too.

If I had a lot of money, though, I guess it would be all right to invest in a big stack of paperback Catholic books. I could just leave them outside the door and never answer the bell, so as not to risk infection, if I had a lot of money.

XIX. THE VALIANT WOMAN

Suppose you do get canonized. You never can tell. God is very, very rich and can supply the money if He pleases. Unless the Sacred Congregation of Rites composes a Mass especially for you, a housewife has a choice of two which may be offered in her honor: the Mass of a Martyr not a Virgin or the Mass of a Holy Woman not a Martyr.

Don't rule out the first one just because you happen to live in suburbia and all your neighbors are friendly and nice. It's applied more frequently than might be suspected, as God delights in doing the improbable as much as the impossible. We know He raised an unsuspecting butcher's wife to this honor. She was Blessed Margaret Clitherow, a mother of three young children. She had friendly neighbors in York, too, but that didn't prevent her being pressed to death for her faith during the reign of Queen Elizabeth. The number of Chinese housewives who may be so honored at this moment may some day shock and surprise us.

Many martyrs have been housewives. Lest we forget it, the Holy Spirit sees fit to mention four of them by name every day in the prayer *Nobis Quoque Peccatoribus* of the Mass. They are St. Perpetua, St. Felicity (who was a slave as well), St. Cecelia and St. Anastasia. "Give thy sinful servants ... some share and fellowship with them!" you pray at least every Sunday. If we get it, we can't say we haven't asked for it.

Barring the palm of martyrdom, most housewives would be well content with the Mass for a Holy Woman which begins, "Cognovi ... I know, O Lord, that thy judgments are equity, and in thy truth thou hast humbled me." Humility is the virtue thrown at the housewife all day long. A housewife who doesn't eventually acquire at least a little could work in a towel factory without picking up lint. And humility, all the saints agree, is facing the truth and living in it.

Luckily for us, how this is done by the housewife is outlined in very practical terms in the Epistle of her Mass. This Epistle is the famous Hebrew alphabetical poem which begins, "Who shall find a valiant woman?" and which occurs at the end of the Book of Proverbs *(31:10-31)*. No housewife serious about her own perfection can afford not to study it.

It was well-known and meditated on by pious Jewesses long before Masses were said, and the Blessed Virgin unquestionably pondered it in her heart. When we consider that it must have contributed powerfully to her growth in holiness in the bosom of the Holy Family where she performed the same chores we do, we can gain some idea of the immensity of its value.

It's a poem full of mystery, and the more you read it, the more mysterious it gets. At first glance, however, it certainly seems plain enough. This Valiant Woman is a real ball-of-fire housekeeper. She's the proverbial one-armed paperhanger from Proverbs, and if she points out the only way to get to heaven, well, you probably haven't got the physical stamina. That's why a superficial reading is so dangerous and why only serious, stable women, preferably with no sense of humor, can stand only one reading.

We find that this paragon of married female virtue is up in the morning before everybody else, in fact "has risen in the night," which is awfully early, and prepares breakfast for family and servants. She spins, she weaves, she keeps the lamps trimmed, she buys real estate and develops it, she farms and plants vineyards, always driving hard bargains—she also feeds the poor and makes clothes for everybody. In her *spare* time, she makes extra linen and a mysterious girdle to sell on the outside and augment the family income, because evidently she has this limitation too.

A recent estimate of the cash value of the average American housewife's services to her family hovers around $200 per week[4]. That's a lot, but hardly news. Writing in the fifth century—B.C., the author of Proverbs says simply, "far and from the uttermost coasts is the price of her." He was inspired by the Holy Spirit.

The Valiant Woman's husband has the good sense to be delighted with her. She enjoys his complete confidence, and why

---

[4] $200 in 1960 is equivalent to $1600 in 2015.

not? Scripture says, "The heart of her husband trusteth in her and he shall have no need of spoils." The word for spoils in the Latin text is *spolium*. It applies to most anything gotten illegally on the outside. The VW's husband obviously needs nothing like that, not even consolation in the local tavern. Nor does he presumably ever have to go out and buy a clean shirt. We understand he "is honorable in the gates, when he sits among the senators of the land." It's clear he's always well got up, his buttons sewed on and his pockets mended. His mind is at rest, because his wife gives him all the emotional stability and self-confidence he needs to get ahead in the world. She doesn't make his evenings unbearable with meaningless chatter, and she doesn't nag, because "she has opened her mouth to wisdom and the law of clemency is on her tongue." She doesn't interrupt his stories and finish them for him, and she never tells tales on him to his associates.

The poem admits guardedly, "he praised her." Every wife knows praise from her husband is the highest praise possible to her in this world. There's nothing harder to get than real praise from someone who knows you as well, and puts up with you as much as a husband does; but when you get it, it's really worth something. The VW got it. Even her children "rose up and called her blessed," and that's the pinnacle.

As I said, her schedule leaves one panting. If I hadn't read this poem more than once before trying to act on it, I might have gone down to an early grave, just trying. I know absolutely nothing about vineyards, let alone girdle making. Thank goodness, on second reading, the symbolism of her chores began to emerge.

In speaking of the Book of Proverbs, St. Jerome mercifully tells us never to stop at the literal sense. In the Encyclical *Spiritus Paraclitus*, Pope Benedict XV quotes him as saying, "Just as we have to seek gold in the earth, for the kernel in the shell, for the chestnut's hidden fruit beneath its hairy coverings, so in Holy Scripture we have to dig deep for its divine meaning." This doesn't mean the literal and obvious meaning isn't true. Certainly the VW was really busy and energetic, capable and efficient, but that's only the beginning.

Reading Scripture is like peeling an onion, I think I read somewhere else. After stripping off the surface meaning, there's always a succession of deeper messages underneath. Rabbinical scholarship—to which St. Jerome was much indebted—recognizes four methods of biblical interpretation. These are *p'shat*, the literal meaning; *d'rash*, the homiletical, which reads for the moral of the story; *remez*, the typological or allegorical, and finally, *sod*, which is the secret meaning given to mystics. How far you penetrate depends on how you pray, how you live, and how serious you are about finding something. Also like onion-peeling, Bible reading may involve a few tears, because it's not for armchair strategists. It's impossible to finish reading the Bible. St. Paul was at pains to tell us that, "All Scripture is inspired by God and useful for teaching, for reproving, for correcting, for instructing in justice; that the man of God may be perfect, equipped for every good work" *(II Tim. 3:16-17)*. It wasn't written for our entertainment.

"Who shall find a valiant woman?" Who indeed? I don't think this question means to imply only that she's rather scarce. (I know several of them.) It's possible the meaning is that she must be *found*, as the Wise Men *found* "the Child with Mary his mother." The Valiant Woman makes herself scarce. Like the Blessed Virgin, she has a habit of disappearing into crowds. She, too, is vulgar.

No one was ever so designed to escape notice—if she so desires—as the housewife. The more her virtues develop, the more she fades into her environment. It's a truism in our *métier*, girls, that the well-kept house rarely causes comment. Whoever notices a clean windowpane? It's only the missing button that attracts attention, not the one just sewed on.

Sanctity is something like good housekeeping, to the eye of the casual observer. It's also like ballet-dancing. The longer and more arduous your training, the more you put your heart in it, and the more you punish your feet inside their slippers, the more effortless and graceful the *entre-chats* appear to the public.

If you don't levitate in the middle of dinner, who's to know you're so holy? Even then, you'll be amazed at what little attention you attract, if you're a housewife. Blessed Anna Maria Taigi, a Roman housewife sometimes consulted by Pope Pius VII, was rather frequently given to raptures of the spirit while at table with the family. At her beatification process, her husband testified that he had found her an absolutely blameless wife. As far as he knew, she had had only one fault. "She was so terribly absent-minded at times," he said. "Who shall find a valiant woman?" is asked in Anna Maria's Mass.

Certainly our poem isn't for clinging vines or ladies who can't balance the checkbook and change a tire on occasion. My friends who know Hebrew tell me the word used for valiant in the original texts is one meaning capable, efficient, with overtones of "worthy of respect." In other words, she's solid, what the French call "*une brave femme*."

St. Jerome, who was pretty tough himself, calls her simply *mulier fortis*, literally, strong woman, because that's what she is. As Grandmother Crane used to say, "You can't be the mother of half a dozen kids and have your wishbone where your backbone ought to be!" Let's say the VW doesn't get to heaven by just drooping in.

"Who shall find a valiant woman? Far and from the uttermost coasts is the price of her.

The heart of her husband trusteth in her, and he shall have no need of spoils.

She will render him good, and not evil, all the days of her life.

She hath sought wool and flax, and hath wrought by the counsel of her hands.

She is like the merchant's ship, she bringeth her bread from afar.

And she hath risen in the night, and given a prey to her household, and victuals to her maidens.

She hath considered a field, and bought it: with the fruit of her hands she hath planted a vineyard.

She hath girded her loins with strength, and hath strengthened her arm."

Strength seems to be a special attribute of hers. The Vulgate renders this last verse, "*Accinxit fortitudine lumbos suos et roboravit brachium suum.*" The verb *roboravit* has *robur* in it, a word which came to mean "oak" to the Romans. St. Thomas put it into the Hymn "*O Salutaris Hostia,*" crying, "*Da robur!*" "Give us strength!"

The Valiant Woman girds her loins, i.e., her maternal functions, with this strength, and she strengthens her arm. She continues to grow even stronger by action. Child-bearing isn't for ninnies, nor is the care of children. Besides, it's one of a woman's main means to heaven. St. Paul made a point of it in his first letter to St. Timothy, noting that, "women will be saved by child-bearing," on condition that "they continue in faith and love and holiness with modesty" *(I Tim. 2:15)*.

And farther on, the poem has, "She hath put out her hand to strong things, and her fingers have taken hold of the spindle." A truly remarkable verse, when you stop to think of it. Only Hebrew poetry, with its talent for balance by contrast, can toy so expertly with apparent contradiction. This was the Jewish way of saying, I suppose, that "The hand that rocks the cradle rules the world."

In other words, she put out her hand, i.e., her whole principle of human action, to accomplishing really great endeavor by setting her fingers, i.e., her small isolated actions, to the spindle. The spindle is of course an almost universal symbol of woman's work in the home. To put it simply, she accomplishes big things by doing little ones. She builds God's kingdom by mending socks. She reaches the eagle's nest at the pace of a hen, obeying the cat and wearing muskrat-dyed mink.

Towards the end, the poem mentions strength again: "Strength and beauty are her clothing." So strength, it would seem, is not a virtue proper only to the male. It's quite compatible with female beauty, especially moral beauty. The poem gives the definite impression that these two qualities are not merely compatible, but that they actually enhance each other, even depending on each other. A housewife shouldn't simper, let's say, just because she's pretty. It'll ruin her looks. Beauty of soul depends on strength of character.

It seems a favorite gambit of the devil in modern times to try to persuade us that "feminine" means frilly and spineless. Antiquity was peculiarly free of this delusion. A real Roman *femina*, certainly, like the matron Lucretia or Cornelia, the mother of the Gracchi, was anything but feminine in the decadent sense of this word. Roman statuary alone would prove that. Only loose women were ever portrayed as soft and squashy, with quivery chins. A woman who produces, nourishes, and educates children simply can't loll, physically or spiritually, or she produces weaklings. If we are to believe Scripture, and we are, strength is so much a feminine attribute, no woman can be feminine without it.

In fact, our collective unconscious so takes this for granted that strength, or courage, which is strength in action, is only rarely noted in women, and then usually by its absence. A case in point might be Gertrud von Le Fort's *Song of the Scaffold*, and Bernanos' play derived from it, *The Fearless Heart*. Sixteen Carmelite sisters face the guillotine during the Reign of Terror, and the entire action revolves around an apparent scandal—the cowardice of one young nun, who nevertheless crashes through gloriously in the end.

Cowardice in women is scandalous. Even physical cowardice. Any mother is supposed to dash into her burning house to save her child. Nobody is surprised when she does. Nobody was surprised at seeing the Blessed Virgin and Mary Magdalene at the foot of the cross. Nobody is surprised at the total gift of self most women make to their families, even very sinful women. Strength and beauty are so much a woman's proper clothing, their absence exposes her to view most shockingly!

The Valiant Woman attires herself becomingly, but she isn't self-centered. We read still further that "She hath looked well to the paths of her house, and hath not eaten her bread idle." This can't just mean she earns her keep and sees that the walks are swept, though I'm sure she does that.

"Paths of her house" opens up a big subject. It leads us to ponder what goes into her house, and what comes out. What visitors does she allow near her children? Who comes to dinner? What TV programs does she turn on? To what magazines does the family subscribe? What comes in through the mail? When do her teen-age children come in from a party? And conversely, what goes out of the house? Soup for a sick neighbor? Contributions for the Society for the Propagation of the Faith? Vocations to religious life? Responsible votes on election day? Letters to the editor? It's a big subject. Looking well to the paths of her house certainly means that she makes it her business to know what's going on within her sphere of authority. It's no wonder she doesn't eat her bread idle. She's probably on the lookout even during meal time.

This might give the impression that her day is even more frenzied than first imagined. Being loaded with moral responsibility far heavier than the big wash, she must be much too busy ever to pray or meditate or read a book. But nothing could be farther from the truth, as we shall see, if we take another layer off the onion.

The poem doesn't say how many paths there were to her house, but my guess is five. A house is a favorite metaphor for the human body. (Even modern poets know that. Was it Edna St. Vincent Millay who called it "this house of bone"?) When the VW "looked well to the paths of her house," she was simply keeping close custody of her senses, through which all temptation, all sacramental life must enter.

This little verse epitomizes her entire ascetical life, which is carried on through the most ordinary events of her day. She takes care what she looks at, what she eats, what she reads, what she listens to, above all, what she says, for she "doesn't eat her bread idle." She must not dissipate God's grace, for her bread is the Bread of Life, the only bread of a valiant woman.

We are also told that "She is like the merchant's ship, and she brings her bread from afar. And she has risen in the night and given a prey to her household." This is her life of prayer, not just a marketing expedition to supply her family. She not only prays for herself, in the night watches, but she delivers the fruits of her prayer to her household.

"She is like the merchant's ship." A truly magnificent phrase! It's all the more magnificent because it's applied to apparently the most humdrum of creatures, the mother of a family. The merchant's ship is always on the high seas, going or coming. Its course on the waters leaves no visible trace. It's a cargo vessel, and the merchant—the Latin calls him *institor*, literally a broker or a huckster—doesn't keep his wares for himself, but trades with them by delivering them to others. The Valiant Woman is no stranger to the prayer of contemplation, the real high seas of the spiritual life, and she bestows the fruits of her prayer on all those with whom she comes in contact. This doesn't mean she spends long hours alone in her room, to the material neglect of her family. She probably does it on the hoof, but like the travel of the merchant's ship, it's pathless, unceasing, and brings bread from afar, the same bread for which we ask in the Lord's Prayer.

This doesn't mean she doesn't sometimes employ more pedestrian means of supplying her family, looking up the habits of the Somaliland klipspringer, for instance, or brushing up on her math, but it does mean she isn't confined to a house with four walls. She lives in Ezechiel's house—the one with the tricky dimensions. She invites St. Augustine to tea simply by discussing him over the teacups. She puts Aristotle into the language of the nursery and teaches moral theology while she relays current events. She seeks afar and gives everyone the benefits of her seeking. Instead of cursing her family with her ignorance, she blesses them with prayer and knowledge, even if this boils down only to helping the children with their homework and their catechism. Maybe she never got through grade school. Maybe she has a Ph.D. What's the difference, if she seeks afar? God has promised that anyone who seeks, finds.

And that brings us to the part about "giving a prey to her household," probably the most mysterious phrase of all. "*Dedit praedam domesticiis suis,*" *Praeda* means specifically spoils of the chase, a quarry of some kind which doesn't just fall into the pot, but which must be hunted up hill and down dale before it's caught. This fruit of long-determined effort is what she gives for the nourishment of her household. You get the definite impression that the Valiant Woman isn't much of a dedicated bridge player or a chain-smoker. In her quiet way, she's always after something, if only a new recipe. In my bones I'm quite certain the prey she gives is Christ, the Fruit of unremitting prayer. He is after all the divine quarry we all chase, and when found, He must be given to others.

He is also the Pearl of great price which the merchant sought after, and it's no coincidence surely that the Gospel of the Holy Woman's Mass specifically mentions this other merchant "seeking good pearls." Her Gospel also includes the passage about "The kingdom of heaven is like unto a treasure hidden in a field; he who finds it hides it, and in his joy goes and sells all that he has and buys that field" *(Matt. 13:44).* This can only be the field the

Valiant Woman "considered" and then bought, and thereupon "with the fruit of her hands she hath planted a vineyard." That field doesn't lie fallow under her ownership. Throughout Scripture the vineyard is a figure of God's chosen people, and in this case can only mean the Valiant Woman's children, whom she plants and tends for God's glory and their eternal happiness.

She is also the householder in her Gospel who "bringeth forth out of his treasure new things and old" *(Matt. 13:52)*, so that, as the poem tells us, "She shall not fear for her house in the cold of snow: for all her domestics are clothed with double garments." This means, I suppose, that she provides them with both physical and spiritual protection against the rigors of the world. The double garment is action and contemplation, the ministrations of Martha supernaturalized by the prayer of Mary.

Not neglecting herself, "She hath made for herself clothing of tapestry: fine linen, and purple is her covering." This is the clothing of a predestined soul. Purple is for the king's daughter. Tapestry is variety, many colored, contrived of thousands of tiny stitches, each individual, but part of a large design. Not to be overlooked is the fact that tapestry must be worked entirely from the underside, the worker never seeing the design until the work is finished. It's the fabric of a life of days. Fine linen, St. John tells us in the Apocalypse, "is the just deeds of the saints" *(19:8)*, and the armies of heaven are clothed in fine linen.

This fine linen, it must be noted, the VW wove with her own hands. She made more than she needed for herself, for "she made fine linen and sold it, and delivered a girdle to the Canaanite." This Canaanite, like the VW herself, is a merchant. In her day, he traded with foreigners, some of them Baal-worshippers, many of them very far away across the then-known seas. So the VW's influence extends a long way outside her home.

For those infidel people unknown to her she weaves linen from the flax which she "wrought by the counsel of her own hands," thereby trading with her very substance. The girdle is very mysterious indeed, but I gather that it was contrived in her spare time, of whatever scraps she happened to have on hand. Its design was probably original with her, and there was a lot of work in it. She may have regarded it as an "outlet" for her creative talents, and put a good deal of artistry in it. It must have been a competent product, or the Canaanite wouldn't have bothered with it. It was probably embroidered, and she amused herself planning the color scheme while she was weaving the fine linen. But just what is this mysterious girdle sold to the outside world? Is it pies for the bake sale? Penance done for missionaries, who are real foraging Canaanites? Is it a chairmanship of the school board which the VW accepts? Does she make vestments? Maybe she publishes a thin volume of esoteric verse?

The girdle must be all those things, but more besides. Dr. Paul Heinisch, the Old Testament scholar, in his book, *Christ in Prophecy*, tells us that, to an Oriental the girdle or broad belt was an important item of clothing. It held his garments in place and added greatly to his appearance. It would have been impossible to picture a person without one. It isn't just a bauble, then, that the VW supplies. It's an essential article of clothing, but it is a thing of beauty, capable of transforming a man's appearance. What she delivers to the outside world through the Canaanite can therefore be nothing less than the life of grace, transmitted through her contacts outside her home.

But one point must be noted: The extra linen was extra linen, and the girdle-making was strictly an overflow activity. I'm sure neither interfered with so much as one unmended sock. They are natural by-products of her life as wife and mother. Can you imagine the VW putting the children in boarding school so she could devote herself entirely to the girdle business? Can you imagine her telling her husband to get himself a sandwich for dinner tonight, "because I've got to finish this girdle for the Canaanite. He'll be here any minute!" Oh, no, for we know "he praised her."

And who is her husband? Where everything is symbol, he must be symbol too. The Tract of the Holy Woman's Mass gives us the clue. It reads, "*Veni, sponsa Christi*—Come, bride of Christ, receive your crown." It is Christ who praises her. Christ is her husband, indissolubly united to her through the Incarnation, and more specially united to her in the sacrament of her Marriage through the visible sign of an earthly relationship.

He praises her, for "Favor is deceitful, and beauty is vain: the woman that feareth the Lord, she shall be praised. Give her of the fruit of her hands: and let her works praise her in the gates!"

And who is the Valiant Woman herself? She is Holy Mother the Church. She is the Blessed Virgin. She is contemplation, and she is every housewife. The verse about her I like best is: "and she shall laugh in the latter day." I think that means that, along with the crown, she gets the LAST LAUGH!

XX. EGGS, AND WHY

St. Anne was a valiant woman, and she's very hard indeed to
find. She's never mentioned at all in Scripture. There's one verse
in St. Luke, however, that proves to me beyond the shadow of a
doubt that she really knew how to bring up a girl. When her
daughter Mary, about fourteen at the time, is confronted quite
suddenly by a celestial being who tells her she is to become the
mother of a son, Mary doesn't argue, but she asks him quite
bluntly, "How shall this happen, since I do not know man?" *(Luke
1:34).*

Any mother baffled by the problems of the sex education of
her children could certainly ponder this verse for hours on end,
trying to reconstruct the excellent home training methods which
must have lain behind it. It's obvious God picked His grandmother
with great care, and that she took her duties very seriously.

She certainly didn't confuse innocence with ignorance. It's
quite evident that the adolescent Mary was well acquainted with
the facts of life and accepted them wholeheartedly and simply as
only the pure can accept them, without any falseness of attitude.
She didn't simper and pretend she didn't know what the Archangel
was talking about. She wasn't scandalized. Nor did she quote from
the high school biology book to prove it couldn't happen.

The angel had just finished saying that this Son was to be
"great and shall be called the Son of the Most High; and the Lord
God will give Him the throne of David His father, and He shall be
king over the house of Jacob forever; and of His kingdom there
shall be no end" *(Luke 1:32-33).*

Staggering as this information was, Mary saw no difficulty
here. What bothered her was a practical obstacle, which she
proceeded to ask about. That she put her question to a superior
angelic being in whose presence a lot of people wouldn't think of
mentioning sex, is just another proof of St. Anne's excellent
pedagogy, and Mary's own absolute purity. The wording of her

question is absolutely straightforward. She didn't stoop to euphemism, poetic or scientific. No birds, no bees, chromosomes or genes. Just, "How? Since I don't know man?"

For his part, the angel evidently considered the question quite proper because he didn't reprove her or disappear indignantly. He answered it, thereby proving a fourteen-year-old has a God-given right to a straight answer to a straight question. "The Holy Spirit," he said, "shall come upon thee and the power of the Most High shall overshadow thee; and *therefore* the Holy One to be born shall be called the Son of God" *(Luke 1:35-36)*. (The force of the *therefore* can be easily overlooked. In it lies hidden the whole mystery of our Lady's virginity, and that of all holy virgins.)

Then the angel went on to tell her that not only would this miracle of virginal motherhood occur, but even her aging and childless cousin Elizabeth was going to have a baby, because, he said significantly, "Nothing is impossible with God." Barren or virgin, by the usual human means or by God's direct agency, procreation is quite simply always an act of God.

The angel thereby put, as it were, the capstone on Mary's sex education begun by St. Anne. Mary accepted the explanation as eminently reasonable and said, again quite matter-of-factly, "Be it done to me according to thy word" *(Luke 1:38)*. Our Lady has a habit, wherever we meet her in Scripture, of choosing always the most ordinary way of doing and saying everything. If she ever sounds stilted, we can be sure it's the fault of the translation or a phrase that won't translate. Though Scripture is inspired, it's comforting to keep in mind that translations ain't necessarily so.

As I say, it's obvious that St. Anne did a very fine job. Just what her exact methods were probably several million mothers would like to know, but thank goodness they don't, because in this branch of human education, cut and dried rules are less use than they are in most places.

To my best recollection, my own sex education began when I asked my mother one day where eggs came from. I was an only child, a city child, and I guess I'd never seen an egg come in anything but a box or a bag, in sets of twelve. She told me. I didn't bother to contradict her, because I figured I could recognize pure fiction when I heard it. Besides, I had long since learned that when

Mother didn't want to tell me something, she didn't want to tell me, and that was that.

So I went and asked great-uncle Ga-Ga (whose real name is Arthur). When he looked rather odd and replied, "Go ask your mother about that," I knew for sure there was some deep secret about eggs that nobody wanted me to know. As for their falling out from under chickens' tails, well, a story like that was an insult to a child's intelligence, and I was indignant. It wasn't even nice! I was, to tell the truth, awfully surprised at Mother. She could have invented some more genteel explanation, or just said she didn't want to tell me, and let it go at that.

I don't know whether this shock constituted low-grade trauma or not, but I think it contributed ultimately to my having five children and moving to an old and inconvenient house in the country, where birth can be seen for the extraordinary thing it is, right from the start. My children would be brought up right!

Well, I didn't make out any better than Mother.

Some twenty-five years later, sitting smack in the middle of the country, surrounded by farmers who raise chickens, pigs, rabbits, cows, and sheep, not to mention the birds, bees, snakes, chipmunks, 'coons, and our own cats, dogs, horses, and the budget-eating goat, my own daughter Lydia asked me, "Mother, where do babies come from?"

I recovered as quickly as possible, and explained as carefully as possible. Lydia listened intently and politely, with her mouth open and her hair in all directions, so attractive to birds. She never interrupted until I had finished. Then she pressed her lips together, curled them and said, "Oh, come on, Mother, tell me the truth! Where do they really come from?"

Obviously skepticism runs in the women of my family, for then began what was probably the most baffling half-hour of my life, when I tried to persuade a child that, fantastic as it may be, children really are born the way they are. Before I was finished, and I was finished, I sincerely wished I had substituted the cabbage-leaf version, because when you stop to think of it, it's a whole lot more believable. I have a sneaking suspicion that the cabbage-leaf story got started in the first place by some cowardly parent in my predicament. Isn't that the way heresy begins? Somebody trying to make mystery plausible?

Well, I didn't back down, and eventually Lydia accepted my version, as pure mystery. She accepted it as all mystery must be accepted, on pure faith, because I crossed my heart. It wasn't until her little brother was born some months later that she admitted I had supporting facts on my side.

That was Tavy, and I vowed that with him, I wouldn't be caught napping. When our current cat, Eloisa, produced a timely litter in the kitchen, I made sure he was in on the *accouchement*. He took it all in stride, and I figured that with boys, if caught early enough, it must be easier to get the idea across. It wasn't. About an hour later, I found him still with Eloisa, just sitting and waiting, staring at the kittens.

"It's all over," I said. "Are you going to sit there all day?" "But, Mommie! Dooze they go back in?"

Don't laugh. Our mental institutions are full of people trying to go back in, figuratively, to the security of the womb. Children know everything first!

One thing they know particularly about sex. They find it hard that it's the same way with humans that it is with cats. They can live around animals for years without necessarily seeing the similarity, and it's not just my children who are obtuse about this. It's a quality of innocence. Learning that we are animals, as rationalists may try to teach them, is humiliating to them. Children know instinctively that we are "different," and it's natural for them to expect this difference to show up physically.

Somehow only a really mature adult, or a child very gifted spiritually, can accept his animal nature in all its plenitude, anywhere near the way in which our Lord accepted it at His Incarnation: "But a body Thou hast fitted to me!" *(Heb. 9:5)*. No imitation of Christ can be entirely spiritual, any more than it can be entirely carnal, because Christ Himself was not entirely spiritual. Mary, who bore Him, knew this better than anyone else.

Teaching a small child the facts of life is a very tricky business, because it opens up for him the whole exasperating dichotomy we live under all our lives as beings composed of matter and spirit. Not matter versus spirit, as Plato and the Puritans would have it.

That would be no problem at all! But matter and spirit. Only God could marry such irreconcilables.

If you teach a child only the physical facts of generation, you aren't teaching the facts of life. You're teaching biology. If you lead him to believe biology is the whole story, you animalize him. If you teach him only the spiritual aspects, dwelling on the false premise that the body is simply a cumbersome vehicle for a soul which is all that matters, you betray our Lord and mock His Resurrection. You Jansenize the child. In both instances you're telling an impressionable little mind a terrible whopper that's much more dangerous than any number of cabbage-leaf tales, and probably paving the way for some of the dandy emotional disorders rampant in society today.

Essentially, every human act is sacramental, or meant to be, and the generative act is no exception. Spiritually we are embedded in matter and must express ourselves in forms and gestures of matter. Human generation is sacramental in the sense that Christ Himself, when He became incarnate, became *the* Sacrament, our very God in, not just flesh, but *our* flesh. He is the Sacrament from which all others derive. Every human birth is an image of the Incarnation, as is every egg in the egg boxes. Every egg is an Easter egg.

When parents teach their children how they came to be born, they teach religion, whether they like it or not. They teach them *their* religion, whatever it is. The mystery they open up for their little ones to contemplate can be resolved ultimately only in the Beatific Vision. Lydia and I, as little girls, found the physical aspects of sex, in themselves, rather silly. Only when these physical aspects can be seen for what they really are—consummate imagery of the Reality which vivifies them—do they make any sense at all.

To teach the facts of life that way is to teach them as St. Anne taught the young Mary. How she did it I have no idea, but of one thing I'm certain. Her teaching didn't depend on a lot of props. It didn't depend on animals, brothers and sisters, or a house in the country, though these can play their part. Although St. Anne and her husband St. Joachim lived in an agricultural society, it doesn't necessarily follow that they kept chickens and had a large family.

As a matter of fact, it's just possible that the Blessed Virgin's childhood environment was rather more like suburbia than latter-day "back to the landers" might care to admit. She lived, we believe, in a small town, and tradition hints strongly that she was an only child of older parents and very proficient in needlework, not animal husbandry.

Apocryphal tales would have us believe she was dedicated to God at a tender age and quite possibly lived in the Temple for a period of time. Perhaps it was in the Synagogue in Nazareth, rather than at home, that the Archangel Gabriel appeared to her. We simply don't know these details. And when Scripture doesn't tell us something we'd very much like to know, it's because it wouldn't do us any good if we did. These circumstances would shed very little light, if any, on the real problem.

The Blessed Virgin's upbringing didn't depend on special circumstances. God gives "special circumstances" to every child. It didn't depend on the Archangel Gabriel, either. It depended on St. Anne. Ay, there's the rub!

St. Anne isn't the patron of Christian mothers for nothing!

XXI. SEX

Frankly I've always been fascinated by sex. I suppose I should say "human love," but this is going to be a vulgar book right up to the last chapter, and human love isn't the same thing as sex. Unfortunately, they can exist separately even when they're not supposed to, because here again we're both body and soul. Nowhere can the effects of the Fall be seen more clearly than here, where soul and body should be integrated but aren't. Even in the dictionary sex and love are made to keep their distance and obey the conventions.

What I really want is a word that means both, and the only word that can mean both is "marriage." In God's plan, any use of sex outside marriage is an anomaly; so I'll take the liberty of using sex, love, and marriage in these few pages interchangeably, as before the Fall.

From now on in, I'll have to be serious, because making jokes about sex can lead only to scurrility, as making jokes about God can lead only to blasphemy. It seems there's absolutely no middle ground. Sex, like God, is sacred. By the same token, dirty jokes are a kind of blasphemy.

Physical details of human love are not often discussed in pious literature for the simple reason that discussing sex is excruciatingly embarrassing to modest people. St. Augustine suffered from this impediment and speculated on why exactly this should be, if sex is good and ordained by God, as we know it is. (In his day, behaviorist psychology wasn't there to obfuscate the issue with "acquired social inhibitions.") In Book XIV of the *City of God* he comes to the conclusion that it's shameful to us because it concerns the bodily powers least under our control as the result of the Fall and therefore the strongest reminder of man's shameful revolt against his Creator.

Certainly our shame is a punishment, which Christ did not neglect to take upon Himself with all the others when He was

132

impaled naked on the Cross. We know our shame didn't exist before the Fall. Although God commanded Adam and Eve to "increase and multiply," Genesis states categorically that "Both the man and his wife were naked, but felt no shame" *(Gen. 2:25)*.

St. Augustine tries to reconstruct what marriage and human procreation must have been like before the Fall, but after a paragraph or so he gives up, saying that modesty shut his mouth, although his mind conceived the matter clearly. Such is the force of the effect of original sin in a great saint and Doctor of the Church.

The problem remains, however, and it's as much the housewife's as the theologian's. Sex lies at the bottom of her entire career, and her perfection is inextricably bound up in it, whether she likes it or not.

Its symbolism is extremely deep. We have St. Paul's word for it that it's "a great mystery." Mysteries are unfathomable because they progressively reveal God. The more we penetrate into them, the more mysterious they become. Any housewife can tell you this is especially true of marriage.

Sex began with Eve's creation. As the old song puts it,

> When Adam was created, he seemed like one alone,
> When to his admiration, he found he'd lost a bone![5]

Or, as Adam himself put it,

> She now is bone of my bone,
> and flesh of my flesh;
> She shall be called Woman,
> for from man she has been taken.

and the inspired author adds, "For this reason a man leaves his father and mother, and clings to his wife, and the two become one flesh" *(Gen. 2:23-24)*.

Thus it seems that in some mysterious way marriage reintegrates the Adam and Eve in every couple and makes them

---

[5] This song can be found in *Laughing Meadows*, ed. By Dr. Jop Pollman, published by Grailville.

one again as they were originally. They are so much one that warfare between them becomes a kind of self-hatred, which would be impossible between any other two human beings. St. Paul says as much in the Epistle of the Nuptial Mass: "Even thus ought husbands also to love their wives as their own bodies. He who loves his own wife, loves himself ... For no man hateth his own flesh" *(Eph. 5:28-29).*

But this is just the outer skin of the onion. The real supernatural mystery hinges on the fact that union of male and female in this life is the image of God's union with the human soul, as it is the image of Christ's union with His bride, the Church. It's an image meant for our instruction which God rooted in our very bones to be felt, lived and understood so plain we couldn't miss it, so profound we could never get to the bottom of it. When He became incarnate, this union "from the beginning" became a Sacrament.

It can be said that each human soul has its first origin in the mind of God as had Eve in Adam's side, and as the Church herself issued from the pierced side of Christ on the Cross. We are meant to be one again in heaven, indissolubly united as are man and wife. It's this that makes divorce, not only illegal, but impossible, in the sense that all sin against God is outside reality. Can we annul the Incarnation by committing mortal sin? Married souls who can't be faithful to each other can't be faithful to God; nor can they be really faithful to each other except through Him. It's all of a piece.

The prophet Osee was the first of the Old Testament authors to use marriage as a figure of the Covenant between God and Israel. He lived in the seventh century B.C., and he got the idea for this from God Himself, who told him, "Go, take thee a wife of fornications. And have of her children of fornications: for the land by fornication shall depart from the Lord" *(Osee 1:2-3).*

So Osee went, Scripture says, "and took Gomer the daughter of Debelaim: and she conceived and bore him a son" *(Osee 1:3).*

Some scholars think that Osee's marriage to an unchaste wife was just so much metaphor. I don't believe it for a minute. Osee could never have written the impassioned book he did unless he had had the actual, heart-rending experience of loving a faithless woman. Only too authentic is the anguish he imputes to God, who is wedded to faithless Israel.

Any sin against God Osee calls "adultery" or "fornication," as does later the prophet Ezechiel. Any infraction of God's law is basically infidelity in the marriage relationship, a special wound to One to whom we are specially and indissolubly bound. Israel, the faithless wife, departs from God: "for she said: I will go after my lovers that give me my bread and my water, my wool and my flax, my oil and my drink" *(Osee 2:5)*.

But soon, says Scripture, "she shall follow after her lovers and shall not overtake them: and she shall seek them and shall not find. And she shall say: I will go and return to my first husband, because it was better with me then, than now" *(Osee 2:7)*.

God takes faithless Israel back, and when Osee speaks of God's forgiveness, more poignant verses can hardly be found in all the Bible. God's forgiveness bespeaks such overwhelming love, and is so unmerited, it can compare in mortal life only with the forgiveness of a husband for his erring wife. She has hurt him as only she can hurt him, and so serious was this offense among the Jews, it was punishable by stoning.

Osee must have known from personal experience how much love forgiveness of this sin requires, when he puts into God's mouth, "Therefore, behold I will allure her and will lead her into the wilderness: and I will speak to her heart ... and it shall be in that day ... *that* she shall call me: My husband" *(Osee 2:14,16)*. And God continues, speaking to us all:

> And I will espouse thee to me forever: and I will espouse thee to me in justice and judgment and in mercy and in commiserations. And I will espouse thee to me in faith: and thou shalt know that I am the Lord.... And I will say to that which was not my people: Thou art my people. And they shall say: Thou art my God" *(Osee 2:19-20,24)*.

Marriage is a love affair. It has to be, because God's union with a human soul, which marriage is meant to reflect, is a love affair. All the saints agree on that point. This basic symbolism of marriage therefore remains true all the way through, right down to the most embarrassing details.

The collection of Hebrew love poems we call the Canticle of Canticles is full of embarrassing details. Beginning, "Let him kiss me with the kiss of his mouth," it goes on from there through a riot of extravagant Oriental imagery that leaves prudes gasping. Saints, who really know what sex is all about, find the Canticle a pretty cold reflection of God's own lovemaking. It's full of yearnings and searchings on the part of a bride for her bridegroom, and the poem yields its meaning only to lovers.

One of these is St. Bernard, who wrote several sermons on the Canticle for his monks. He comments on this first line:

> *Let Him kiss me with the kiss of His mouth.* Who speaks? The bride. Who is she? The soul thirsting for God. I now put before you various dispositions of soul so that the one which is especially suited to a bride may shine forth more clearly. If one is a servant, he is in dread of his lord's face. If one is a hireling, he is in dread of his lord's hand. If one is a disciple, he gives ear to his teacher. If one is a son, he honors his father. But the soul who begs a kiss, is in love!
>
> Among the gifts of nature this affection of love holds first place, especially when it makes haste to return to its first origin, which is God. Words cannot be found so sweet as to express the sweet affections of the Word and the soul for each other, except bride and bridegroom. For persons so related, all things are held in common. There is nothing that one can appropriate as his own, nothing that one can divide so that the other is excluded from a share. Both have one inheritance, one home, one table, even one flesh.
>
> On this account, "a man shall leave father and mother, and cleave to his wife: and they shall be two in one flesh."

In the Canticle's third poem the bridegroom says of the bride, "My sister, *my* spouse, is a garden enclosed, a fountain sealed up" *(4:12)*. It's a beautiful passage often applied to our Lady, God's chosen spouse, in praise of her virginity, but this is only one of its meanings. Its fundamental meaning harks back to "the beginning" when "God took the man and placed him in the garden of Eden to till it and to keep it" *(Gen. 2:15)*. Man's first and basic occupation, it would seem, is that of a gardener. It's his function to plant the earth and make it produce. This function is his spiritually also and explains why only men can be priests. Is it mere whimsy that our Lord, the exemplar of cultivators of souls, was mistaken by Mary Magdalene after His Resurrection as "the gardener"!

Man is also a gardener in the marriage-bed, because his union with his wife represents the union of God and the soul, a relationship of gardener with garden. He is given his garden "to till and to keep" when he promises to love, cherish, and protect his wife.

In all literatures and mythologies, the earth is the figure of woman. Under countless names, Ceres, the earth goddess, is a universal symbol of fertility. With sure instinct, St. Ephrem the Syrian, who was a poet, didn't hesitate to call our Lady "the garden upon which descended from the Father the rain of benedictions ... God's Eden," he said, "is Mary."

Woman's role in the marriage act is passive, but not inert, any more than the human soul before God. She is meant to be aroused to response as a garden responds to the gardener. Oh, if only modern men in our secular world could be made to pore over gardening manuals and seed catalogues when tempted to read those ghastly sex books purveying mutual masturbation! If only they would pray and read Scripture! What they wouldn't learn about sexual "compatibility"! Unfortunately, the people most qualified to write sex books could never bring themselves to do so. Modesty shuts their mouths, but rarely shuts the mouths of fools. As long as there is religion without theology, there can be sex without love.

Now, this is a book about housewives. A housewife was created "a helper like himself" *(Gen. 2:15)* for Adam. That means she'll see that his suits get to the cleaners, she'll do his official entertaining, and run the house and children while he battles the world, but that's not all. She's supposed to be a helper spiritually also. She may bear him twenty-two children and lecture him on his faults every day, but if he doesn't reach God, she will have failed in one of her most important duties.

I see a curious thing: One of the most powerful ways a woman can bring her husband to God is through the marriage act. Let me explain. Woman, we have seen, is easily "contemplative." The main reason women fill churches, even when the men have fled, is that women are naturally disposed to come to God, living more within themselves. They are also more passive, dependent, endowed with a natural urge to complete themselves by giving themselves. Also, they are one step removed from carnality to begin with, by reason of Eve's having been created from Adam, and not directly from "the slime of the earth" as he was. They are the weaker, both physically and rationally, but they are the more spiritual sex. They are more intuitive and have more heart than head, love more than they know. That's not being inferior. Theology tells us that although we must have knowledge to love, love takes you much further.

Man is not these things by nature. To reach God, his soul must, spiritually speaking, become feminine before God's advances. It must become the bride of the Canticle. For most men, this is extremely difficult. Their entire nature resists it. Small wonder that fewer men than women have been great contemplatives.

How is the average man, the vulgar man, to learn such "high" wisdom? From his wife, through his own carnality, in the physical act of love. Nowhere is the sacramentality of sex more clearly seen. In its perfection, the role of the woman in love is perfect response, perfect self-giving, trust, affection, obedience—all the things God asks of us. From her, her husband can learn these dispositions.

The lesson she teaches, for the most part quite unconsciously, makes use of many seemingly unimportant details completely understood only by saints. St. John of the Cross, the Church's great doctor of mystical theology and one of the world's most impassioned poets, attempted to put God's love-making into words. The result is some of the most famous lines in all spiritual literature. They are so beautiful; they sound good even if you don't understand them:

> ¡Oh, llama de amor viva,
> Que tiernamente hieres
> De mi alma en el más profundo centro!
> Pues ya no eres esquiva,
> Acaba ya si quieres
> Rompe la tela de este dulce encuentro,[6]

It helps, of course, to be a Spaniard! Being a saint as well, St. John here makes use of very bald, very pure sexual imagery. The soul, represented as enamored and purified by God's previous intermittent advances, says in simple language, "Now You are no

---

[6] Spanish translation: "Oh, it calls of a living love/That hurts so tenderly/From my soul in its deepest center/Then you are no longer elusive/It ends now if you want it to/It breaks the fabric of this sweet encounter"

longer playing hard-to-get, come, consummate our union. Break the web of this sweet encounter!" Only saints can speak to God like that. To imperfect souls, it's bound to sound scandalous.

The web of this life, which separates us from the full possession of God, is, in the analogy of sex, quite simply the hymen. Death is the painful rending which will give us eternal happiness. The consummation of the marriage act, therefore, can be nothing less than an earthly image of the soul's encountering the Beatific Vision.

This imagery is so apt, so precise in all its ramifications, it's small wonder saints hardly have to be told the facts of life. No one, it seems, ever told the Little Flower, who entered the convent at fifteen, but from her knowledge of God's ways in prayer, she "just knew." Perhaps it had been this way with our Lady, whose instruction from St. Anne was simply instruction in the ways of God. "The spiritual man," says St. Paul, "judges all things." Light from above illumines everything below it.

Small wonder sex is sacred. Sex and prayer go together and mutually reveal each other. No one fascinated by God could fail to be fascinated by sex. The young Tobias and his wife Sara, whom Scripture presents to us as patterns for newlyweds, prayed for three days before consummating their marriage, because they understood very well that "we are the children of saints, and we must not be joined together like heathens that know not God!" *(Tob. 8:5)*.

Indeed not, for Tobias had received pre-marital instruction from no less a person than the Archangel Raphael. Isn't it remarkable the way archangels seem to figure as interpreters of the higher aspects of sex? He told Tobias, "For they who in such manner receive matrimony, as to shut out God from themselves, and from their mind, and to give themselves to their lust, as the horse and the mule, which have not understanding, over them the devil hath power" *(Tob. 6:17)*.

Is it possible that a lot of modern sex books are written for horses and mules, who can't read? We are evidently expected to exercise our understanding concerning sex, unlike the animals. The spiritual truths hidden in marriage can reveal themselves only to spiritual beings, who find them mirrored mysteriously in their own flesh.

I can't pursue the subject further. Sex, like prayer, must be engaged in secretly and humbly, for by divine decree it is now shielded from earthly view.

"Who told you that you were naked?" *(Gen. 3:11)* the Lord God asked Adam and Eve in their fig leaves, hiding among the trees after their sin.

XXII. ADAM AND EVIL

I read somewhere that the Orthodox Church sings the "Chant of the Holy Martyrs" at wedding processions. It's not a bad idea, because it introduces right away the spice every romance needs to keep it from getting sickening.

To see how apt this custom is we must, however, put martyrdom in proper perspective. It isn't always bloody and necessarily accompanied by the "sighing of the prisoners." A martyr is simply a witness, that being what the word means. Every Christian is supposed to be a martyr, and his martyrdom will take the special form designed just for him. Its form will be all the nasty things that happen to him, in spite of which he will still cling to God and witness thereby his faith in Christ. You may have to let an Indian chew your fingers, but more likely you'll just have to let your husband keep that awful chair in the living room day after day.

The French Dominican Father Roguet, who has done much research on the Sacrament of Marriage, calls Christian marriage "a mystery of death, a total giving, abnegation for the individual." The general form taken by this death of self for married people is clearly laid out for Adam and Eve by Almighty God right after their disobedience. It wasn't meant to be this way, but it's the only way out now. God tells Adam,

> Cursed be the ground because of you; in toil shall you eat of it all the days of your life;
> Thorns and thistles shall it bring forth to you, and you shall eat the plants of the field.
> In the sweat of your brow you shall eat bread, till you return to the ground,
> Since out of it you were taken; for dust you are and unto dust you shall return *(Gen. 3:18-19).*

In other words, husbands have to work hard for a living, bearing disappointment and frustrations of all kinds, and eventually die. As a "helper like unto himself," Eve gets her share of this. It accounts for washing machines overflowing, crocuses that didn't come up, and why the house or the children won't stay clean. Not being a husband, I can't expatiate on men's difficulties, but I'm willing to believe theirs is a lot as hard as the housewife's. Well, almost.

Her punishment has some extra refinements. God tells her, "I will make great your distress in child-bearing; in pain shall you bring forth children!" *(Gen. 3:16)*. This needs little elaboration, if you're a mother. It begins with morning-sickness, takes in the humiliation of a baggy maternity dress (the good one is always at the cleaners), goes through the actual birth pains right on to the patter and CHATTER of childhood, music lessons, the first failure on the report card, and includes all the free theatre tickets you pass up because you can't get a sitter. I haven't reached the end yet, myself, so I can't give you the whole picture.

It's the next two lines that may need a little developing: "For your husband shall be your longing, though he have dominion over you" *(Gen. 3:16)*. For me, these two lines are loaded. They contain in germ all of a woman's most interior sufferings, all her psychological disbalances, her "nerves." They involve her right to vote, Carrie Nation, frigidity, trips to the beauty parlor, much of the Kinsey report, and why the best cooks always turn out to be men.

Almighty God punishes us not only to satisfy His justice, (which we can't do of ourselves anyway), but in order to turn us to Him. In His punishments lie buried not only satisfaction; for the fault committed, but a remedy for the fault itself and an increase of grace.

Adam finds redemption applied to him via thorns and thistles, made supernaturally fruitful by Christ, who endured them too. Thorns and thistles are a peculiarly appropriate punishment for Adam, because his sin was a sensual, affective sin. He disobeyed God with full knowledge. He ate the fruit of the tree because he realized only too well the terrible thing Eve had done, foresaw the consequences, and couldn't bear to be parted from her.

Theologians speculate that if Adam hadn't partaken, Eve's sin would probably have fallen only on herself, not on us. It is in his role as head of the human race that Adam transmits sin to his descendants. When he wobbled, all visible creation wobbled with him, a cataclysm endlessly repeated in miniature in every family where the husband is unsteady.

Eve is after all responsible for just so much! But getting blamed for Adam's defections is another of her woes. "The woman you placed at my side gave me fruit from the tree and I ate" *(Gen. 3:12)*, Adam informs God. (Chivalry died before it began.) He even has the effrontery to hold God Himself more than a mite responsible, for having given him Eve in the first place. Haven't we heard it's always women who drive men to drink?

Trying to accept undeserved blame gracefully is part of Eve's martyrdom, but we needn't pity her too much. As you will remember, she tried to pin the blame on the serpent. In order to understand Eve's punishment, it's necessary to understand her sin, too. It wasn't a sin of sense. It was a sin of pure pride, and intellectual pride at that. (That's why I worry about longing for the works of Tertullian. He died a hot and heavy heretic, you know.)

The serpent wasn't born yesterday. He came to her and told her if she ate the fruit, she would "be like God, knowing good and evil" *(Gen. 2:5)*. Now, the serpent knew better than to tempt Adam with a story like that. He got Eve off by herself and tempted her, because reason isn't her strong point. (Wait! It's true! I'll explain later.) Not only did she rely on her own judgment and go ahead and eat, not bothering to consult Adam; she tried to fix everything by dragging him into the act, contrary to his full understanding of what was involved. Never underestimate the power of a woman—over a man!

When we consider, however, what beauty Eve must have possessed in the fullness of her *"natura integra"* before the Fall, the perfection of her physical and spiritual union with her husband, and the fact that she was literally the only woman in the world for him, well, we have to admit Adam was sorely tried. He sinned because he simply couldn't face life without the helper God created especially for him. "This thing is bigger than both of us," he probably said, caving in.

Eve sinned because she got above herself, like Lucifer the serpent. She wanted to exercise her intellect on her own, outside

Adam's authority, and consequently she misjudged badly. She forgot she was taken from Adam's side and that but for him, there was no reason for her existence. "For man was not created for woman," says St. Paul, "but woman for man" *(I Cor. 11:10)*. A hard saying, if you're a woman. I heard a teen-age boy say once, "You know, if I'd been born a girl, I'd shoot myself!" Well, that's out, if you're heading for heaven. All woman's perfection in marriage hangs on understanding and accepting St. Paul's unvarnished truth.

"For your husband shall be your longing," said Almighty God, "though he have dominion over you" *(Gen. 3:16)*. This dependence on her husband isn't just financial and sensual. It's also spiritual. Eve's sanctification, like anybody else's, must lie precisely where it hurts most. She can't do without a man, and if she's not careful, she hates him and herself for it. Through the centuries she pays for her disobedience by being obedient, for her pride by submitting to humiliation. In her lies always her first sin: the subtle temptation to despise her husband. It's the primordial "I will not serve!" of Satan, transmitted to her by the envious serpent.

It usually comes disguised, of course: the urge to influence her husband's judgment arbitrarily, to set hers up against his; resentment of his freedom in the world; catering to his carnality and then feeling superior to him because of it. Frequently, her natural talents are such as to appear to justify her being the "real" head of the family. Hogwash! Eve thought so too and broke the sacramental bond of God's order, plunging the whole world into misery. This bond is still more important than what bills to pay, where you live, or what pictures go on the walls. A housewife must obey her husband and still manage to love and respect him. That's her dichotomy to resolve, and galling to pride it is, because God meant it to be.

The devil knows Eve very well, far better than she knows herself, particularly in her fallen state where everything's gone haywire. She hates to face the fact that her reason operates fully only when submitted to authority, that she was created "a helper" and that her vocation lies there and there only. Because she is destined to be a helper, she is given a genius for the practical, for implementing the theories Adam thinks up. She has rich instincts and emotions.

I hope I won't be considered a complete traitor to my sex if I quote the following lines from the Diary of Father Alexander Yelchaninov, a Russian Orthodox priest. He has theology on his side, and he also happened to be married, so his knowledge isn't just speculative:

> Woman has been call "a vessel of infirmity." This "infirmity" consists especially in her enslavement to the natural, elementary forces within and outside herself. Result: inadequate self-control, irresponsibility, passion, blind judgments. [OW!] Scarcely any woman is free of the latter; she is always the slave of her passions, of her dislikes, of her desires. In Christianity alone does woman become man's equal, for then she submits her temperament to higher principles and develops sound judgment, patience, logic, wisdom. Only then does friendship with the husband become possible.

Hard to swallow, but Holy Mother our Church would seem to endorse the Russian Father's opinion. The long prayer said over the bride and groom at the Nuptial Mass is almost entirely a plea for God's protection of the woman against her own weaknesses. It reads:

> ... look graciously upon this handmaid of Thine, now to be joined in wedlock, who begs for the safeguard of Thy protection. Upon her let the yoke be one of love and peace. Let her marriage, under Christ, be chaste and true; and let holy matrons ever be her pattern. May she be, like Rachel, dear to her husband; like Rebecca, prudent; like Sara, faithful and long-lived. Let no action of hers give the Father of Lies dominion over her; but let her ever remain steadfast in the faith and Thy commandments, true to one marriage-bed, shunning forbidden embraces, and strengthening her weakness by firm discipline; of grave demeanor, held in honour for her modesty, well-schooled in heavenly lore. May she be fruitful in offspring. May her life be one of tried and proven innocence; and may she come to rest among the blessed in Thy heavenly kingdom.

Her husband's weaknesses aren't even mentioned, let alone prayed for!

God doesn't consider woman hopeless, however. Far from it. He decreed that a woman should be the instrument of the serpent's downfall. Because Satan tempted a woman to sin, his punishment, too, must fit his crime. God tells him, "I will put enmity between you and the woman, between your seed and her seed; He shall crush your head, and you shall lie in wait for His heel" *(Gen. 3:15)*. The Mother of the serpent's Conqueror was the wife of a man called Joseph, who had dominion over her.

"Behold the handmaid of the Lord," she said. "Be it done to me according to Thy word" *(Luke 1:38)*.

XXIII. OLD LADIES

A couple of years back I bumped into a Chinese girl called Mei-Mei. She said she came from Hong Kong and that her name meant Little Sister. We got to talking.

"My," she said at one point, "you don't look old enough to have a son in college!"

I was horrified. "Mei-Mei," I looked her straight in the eye, "what's your little game? You aren't Chinese at all!"

"Why, certainly I am!" (She did *look* Chinese.)

"No real Chinese would ever tell me such a thing. At least not to my face! You would have put it, 'Oh, you look much too *old* to have a son still in college!'" I've been around.

She laughed. "Oh, that's true. In my country I'd never dare, but I've been here long enough to know it's a terrible insult to call anyone old in America. That was one of the first things I learned. It was awful until I did," she reminisced ruefully. "It seems very odd to us, you know."

I know. I can also imagine how she must have put her foot in it, because it's happened to me. I had lived in Mei-Mei's part of the world only a short time, but when I came home I too pulled the unforgivable blunder of referring to some old ladies as "old ladies." I didn't to their faces, thank goodness, but somebody told them, and believe me, the sequel hasn't been easy.

The Western attitude toward age doesn't puzzle just the Chinese. It puzzles me too. I would have been happy to apologize to the o-- ladies, but I couldn't figure how to put it. "I'm sorry you're old?" That would hardly mend matters; besides, I'm *not* sorry. "I'm sorry I called you old?" That makes no sense. Being old isn't like having buck teeth or being a miser.

Holy or not, every housewife who lives long enough is bound to become old. It's part of her vocation. For her, it's the full-flowering of wisdom, when, rooted in God, anything she pleases to say edifies her hearers. She lets her hemline drop and her waistline stay put and adjusts her bifocals to a wider horizon.

At least that's the impression I get from Scripture. Dealing with wisdom as they do, the Sapiential Books especially teem with praise of age and make some snide remarks about silly youth.

"In the ancient is wisdom, and in length of days prudence," remarks Job *(12:12)*.

Ecclesiasticus asks testily, "What doth he know, that hath not been tried? A man that hath much experience, shall think of many things: and he that hath learned many things, shall show forth understanding.

"He that hath no experience, knoweth little: and he that hath been experienced in many things, multiplieth prudence.

"He that hath not been tried, what manner of things doth he know? He that hath been surprised, shall abound with subtlety" *(34:9-11)*.

And again, "Despise not the discourse of them that are ancient and wise, but acquaint thyself with their proverbs" *(8:9)*.

Wisdom makes clear that wise and holy youth is out of the order of nature, a supernatural phenomenon. She speaks of the just man who dies young as "being made perfect in a short space, he fulfilled a long time" *(Wis. 4:13)*, time in his case having been telescoped by God's grace.

"Old age is a crown of dignity," says Proverbs *(16:31)*, siding with the Chinese.

To tell you the truth, these being my confessions, I can't wait to be an old lady. I can't wait to have some young whippersnapper in a flashy skirt tell me I don't look a day over thirty-five, but my usefulness is gone. I aim to turn off my hearing aid and point out to her that it was an Old Lady who was assumed into Heaven. It was an Old Widowed Housewife, I'll say, who was crowned there as Queen of Angels and Saints, and not some inexperienced little ninny of a girl who knew nothing and hadn't suffered!

I'll soon be forty, and I've got a speech all prepared, peppery with telling quotations. I've worried about the aging process to the point of doing a little research, and in the following pages I'm passing on what I've found so far, quotations and all, in case you're worried too. You can go on from there.

Here as elsewhere, the only real help is to be found in Scripture, where theory fastens securely into flesh and you can get hold of it. As St. Paul said, "The word of God is living and efficient, keener than any two-edged sword, and extending even to the division of soul and spirit, of joints also and of marrow." Arthritic joints? Well, why not?

For instance, I suppose it's part of our Western worship of immaturity to overlook the fact that the Blessed Virgin was at least sixty-three or sixty-four years old before she achieved her full spiritual stature and completed her work on earth. The Acts of the Apostles paint an opening scene in a famous upper room where "All ... with one mind continued steadfastly in prayer with the women and Mary, the mother of Jesus" *(1:14)*, awaiting the fire and wind of Pentecost.

This mature Mary, now free from family chores, was hardly there by accident. Can anyone estimate her influence on the infant Church, which she grandmothered as surely as she mothered the Baby Christ—or the stores of human experience and wisdom she must have laid humbly at its disposal? Could a young woman have commanded the respect necessary for this task? Her personal maturity was inextricably bound up with the development of her earthly mission, as it is with all of us. God hardly wills young ladies to become old ladies for no reason, any more than fruit forms without flowers.

Proverbs capsulizes the essential difference between youth and age in an incomparable verse: "The joy of young men is their strength: And the dignity of old men, their grey hairs" *(20:29)*.

Now, there's a French proverb that expresses the same idea a bit less decorously. Something like Justice Holmes' "Oh, to be sixty again!" it goes further and twits,

> *Si jeunesse savait!*
> *Si vieillesse pouvait!*

"If youth only knew, if age only *could!*"

This is solid. Like Popeye's slogan, it's wistful and profound. It puts both youth and age in their place. To youth is given power; to age is given wisdom. Neither may appropriate the other's gift, yet the destiny of the world depends on their full cooperation. When they don't cooperate, we have lopsided families, a lopsided society, and lopsided people. If each doesn't make use of its gift at the proper time, we develop oldsters with nothing to impart and youngsters who won't listen anyway. We get a situation like the one in America today, where we gasp in horror at Eskimos who put useless grandparents out on the ice to die because the food supply is low, but think nothing of putting ours out of sight in institutions because they make nuisances of themselves at our parties.

Social critics advance many complicated theories to explain our fear of old age. At the housewife's level, however, there's nothing complicated about it. A housewife doesn't want to get old because she doesn't want to be relegated to an institution, or laughed at, or humored like a child, or hated, or treated the way she treats old people. And, to put it bluntly, she may not want to become like the old people she knows.

If she's worldly, she doesn't want to end up exuding all the fresh allure of an embalmed corpse in pancake make-up and pale blue hair, her varicose veins sheathed in sheer nylons as she imparts distilled wisdom at a favorite cocktail bar. It's a dreaded time of life when vices once rather attractive in the stage-dressing of youth now stand out in unmitigated ugliness. A "magnificent temper" shaking beautiful young red locks is just vile temper when the locks are gray. Vanity in Miss America may find excuses in its beholders, but the same vanity in a chicken-headed crone finds only derision.

On the other hand, if the housewife is devout, she doesn't want to become what the French call a *punaise d'église*. I hate to drag the French in all the time, but they do have a gift for pungent expression. This choice phrase, meaning literally "church-bug," is applied to a species of ancient female which literally infests churches, hopping around sanctuaries, clad in flea-black, forever mumbling prayers and burning candles and being as poisonous as possible on the outside. Even in church they are characterized by an insane attachment to particular pews and particular duties, and become violent when dislodged. (I must refer you to M. Francois

Mauriac for further information on *punaises*, as the subject is too ramified for this small volume.)

Alas, being old doesn't automatically make us holy or wise. Although "Old age is a crown of dignity," Proverbs is careful to add, "when it is found in the ways of justice" *(16:31)*. It's true old friends may be like old wine, but old wine is just a step from the rawest vinegar. That's what makes growing old so dangerous, and why a housewife has to be so careful.

Sanctity or vinegar? This is important, and it all boils down to being your own grandma. As Ecclesiasticus puts it, "The things that thou hast not gathered in thy youth, How shalt thou find them in thy old age?" *(25:3)*. This means an old lady must begin being an old lady as soon as possible, while she's still a young lady with that "power."

Spiritual growth, thank God, is independent of physical decay. Logically, growing old should alarm only materialists, Communists, and atheists who expect to disappear with their own bodies. For Christians, aging is progressing. A humble young redhead can become an even humbler grayhead. Patience is beautiful in youth, but even more beautiful in old age, where it stands out alone without those distracting dimples. For though our vices are more apparent in old age, so are our virtues. Perfected as they should be, they transform and illumine our flesh in anticipation of the final transfiguration to come.

Again, this is best summed up by Ecclesiasticus, which gets my vote as The Old People's Handbook. (I'm truly sorry Protestants consider it apocryphal.) Speaking of perfect womanhood, it says, "As the lamp shining upon the holy candlestick, so is the beauty of the face in a ripe age" *(26:22)*. This is the beauty our Lady must have achieved when she was assumed into Heaven, a beauty that goes all the way through. Theology tells us it can even be said to have been a very condition of her Assumption. Her flesh partook so perfectly of her fullness of grace; its corruption was literally impossible.

Ecclesiasticus also counsels old people about talking too much: "Speak, thou that art elder; for it becometh thee. To speak the first word with careful knowledge: and hinder not music. Where there is no hearing, pour not out words: and be not lifted up out of season with thy wisdom" *(32:4-6)*.

Can anything compare with our Lady's silence at Pentecost? Apparently she spoke less and less as she grew older, and after her "Do whatever He tells you" at Cana, no speech of hers is recorded at all. Mature wisdom, it would seem, is not necessarily transmitted by talk!

In his little Epistle to Titus, St. Paul limns for us old ladies a model that might transform the world if imitated. He thinks they should "be marked by holiness of behavior not slanderers nor enslaved to much wine; teaching what is right, that they may train the younger women to be wise, to love their husbands and their children, to be discreet, chaste, domestic, gentle, obedient to their husbands so that the word of God be not reviled" *(2:3-5)*.

This is a big order. Not only must old ladies avoid their number one failing —ugly gossip —they mustn't tipple and they must be saints. He also makes it plain that the old lady's mission is apostolic. She transmits Christian tradition by teaching and being an example to younger ones, thereby contributing to the holiness of the Church. She is designed by God to give others the benefit of her experience and help them over the rough spots she once stumbled over. She mustn't give old age a bad name, but must be so holy and wise, the young ladies won't be able to wait to become old!

Is there any part of the Kinsey Report, aside from the statistics, that a wise old grandmother couldn't have acquainted us with? Especially the most important part—the missing section which could only be supplied by those who refused to be interviewed? Unfortunately, grandmothers aren't statisticians or endowed by foundations, so they continue out of favor in America.

"A wise son heareth the doctrine of his father, But he that is a scorner heareth not!" *(Prov. 13:1)*. Now, not all of us are scorners. Could the shoe be on the other foot? Could it be that we must have Kinsey Reports because grandmother has fallen down on the job? In times past, old people supplied the major part of the laity's spiritual direction, along with the Sacrament of the Present Moment and the Cat. If this is no longer true, it could be that few old people now reach full maturity and are simply not equipped to guide anyone.

The fact remains that Redemption itself could hardly have come to us without the full cooperation of myriads of old people from Abraham and Sarah on down to the aged Simeon and Anna, who alone were spiritual enough to recognize the infant Messias when He entered His temple for the first time. Nowhere is this role of age better glimpsed than in the great Mystery of the Visitation. It reveals so beautifully the fundamental relationship of youth and age, which makes possible the orderly progression of history and the transmission of human culture.

Immediately after the Annunciation, the young Virgin Mary, bearing in her womb the Redeemer Himself, runs "in haste" (being young and limber) to her old cousin Elizabeth, who is bearing the last of the Prophets. When she salutes Elizabeth at the door of the house, the Church greets the Synagogue, and the New Testament embraces the Old. "Mercy and justice," the young housewife and the old housewife, "have kissed," just as the Psalmist said they would.

Elizabeth, "being filled with the Holy Spirit," says humbly to her young relative, "Blessed art thou among women and blessed is the fruit of thy womb!

"And how have I deserved that the mother of my Lord should come to me? For behold, the moment that the sound of thy greeting came to my ears, the babe in my womb leapt for joy. And blessed is she who has believed, because the things promised her by the Lord shall be accomplished" *(Luke 1:42-45)*.

Elizabeth hadn't become overnight the sort of old lady who can prophesy like this. Obviously, she must have trained to be an old lady from the cradle, for we are told she was "just before God, walking blamelessly in all the commandments of the Lord."

Marvelling at her, Mary replies with the Magnificat. "My soul magnifies the Lord," she begins, knowing her cousin understands such things. Then she continues,

> ... and my spirit rejoices in God my Savior;
> Because he has regarded the lowliness of his handmaid;
> for, behold, henceforth all generations shall call me blessed
> Because he who is mighty has done great things for me,

> and holy is his name;
> And his mercy is from generation to generation on those who fear him.
> He has shown might with his arm,
> he has scattered the proud in the conceit of their heart.
> He has put down the mighty from their thrones, and has exalted the lowly.
> He has filled the hungry with good things, and the rich he has sent away empty.
> He has given help to Israel, his servant, mindful of his mercy
> Even as he spoke to our fathers
> to Abraham and to his posterity forever *(Luke 1:46-55)*.

What a beautiful scene! Every young woman with an old friend can bask in its light. It lies at the core of human living: in a house in a small town for one enchanted moment the sacramental character of human relationships is exposed to full view.

Scripture tells us "Mary remained with Elizabeth about three months." Presumably she lent young enthusiasm and sturdy arms and legs—her "power" —to preparations for the great Preparer himself, St. John the Baptist. *Jeunesse pouvait*, and did.

But what does Elizabeth contribute in return? Her "wisdom" of course. *Vieillesse savait*, and imparts. As an older female relative, standing perhaps in the place of St. Anne, who tradition implies was deceased at this time, what motherly advice does Elizabeth give to Mary?

Let's remember the Blessed Virgin was in a very awkward and compromising position at the time. She didn't even tell St. Joseph about her coming motherhood. God, however, didn't leave her without human support. Taking her cue from the Angel's startling information about her cousin, Mary rightly judged that Elizabeth was in some mysterious way involved in the great secret and could be confided in. She runs to her for guidance and reassurance as much as to share in her happiness and to offer her help.

We don't know what Elizabeth's advice was, but we do know everything turned out all right. It's fun to speculate on what housekeeping hints and wifely wisdom Mary may have picked up "in the hill country" to the future benefit of St. Joseph and the Word made Flesh. But then, doesn't God always stand at the end of human knowledge? Even "How to Can Spiced Pears" must end in Him, and in this case it must in very fact have done just that.

Anyway, what a mercy for us Elizabeth hadn't been retired to some fancy institution!

XXIV. LAST OF ALL...

I've got this far and just read over what I've written. I wonder how I ever had the nerve. I appreciate now how hard it is to bare the heart.

Besides, I can see the Pharisees closing in on me—in perfect justice here—as they did on the "man born blind" healed by our Lord.

"Thou wast altogether born in sins, and dost thou teach us?" *(John 9:34)* they glare.

Oh, dear.

Behind them stands Job. He asks, "Hath God any need of your lie, that you should speak deceitfully for Him?" *(Job 13:7).*

And behind Job, almighty God thunders from the whirlwind, "Who is this that wrappeth up sentences in unskillful words?" *(Job 38:2).*

Oh, dear. Oh, dear.

I can only answer the same thing the man born blind did:

"All I know is, whereas I was blind, now I see!" *(John 9:25).*

I might add, shakily, that I've spared my readers the story of my conversion, which is just as fascinating as anybody else's, but my real defense can come only from our Lord, who defends all those once blind, as He did the young man. "For judgment have I come into this world," said He, "that they who do not see may see, and they who see may become blind" *(John 9: 39).*

So here I am, much like the orator I heard about once who habitually approached any subject of which he was ignorant by announcing he would deliver a series of lectures on it. You learn a lot that way, and after this much, I begin to understand why St. Thomas never bothered to finish the *Summa.* "It's just a little straw," he sighed. There are some subjects that are simply too big to be finished, and this one is much too big for me.

It's really time I stopped, anyway. Since I started, the baby has gotten to be two years old, lightning has struck, Stephen has sprouted front teeth, I've burned both legs in a brush fire, and our oldest son—the one who talks to cats—has entered the novitiate.

What's more, my husband has had time to go to Tunis and back where a streetcar (actually an interurban) named La Marsa Plage takes one to Carthage. It was in the amphitheatre in Carthage that St. Vibia Perpetua, one of those housewives mentioned in the Canon of the Mass, was martyred. My husband says I'd better be careful. Perpetua got an urge to write, too, and she didn't stop until her dying day.

Scribbling in prison under creative limitations that would put mine to shame, Perpetua left us a wonderful, lively account of her martyrdom right up to the last minute. It's full of "he saids" and "I saids," written as only a woman could, discussing her father, her visions, and how she managed to nurse the baby, all in the same breath. A well-born, egghead housewife who spoke Greek fluently, Perpetua nevertheless chose to write it all in Latin, the vulgar tongue, and she produced an eminently vulgar story, delightful to read. My husband bought me a copy—in Latin.

Though highly educated, Perpetua was no Doctor of the Church, heaven knows. As a matter of fact, she was only a catechumen when she was apprehended, but she possessed the faith unto the shedding of her life's blood. She was especially careful to preserve a housewife's most valuable asset: her amateur standing in all fields.

When anybody thinks he's pretty good at anything, he yearns to be a professional. It's a standing temptation. The Pharisees were professionals. The real reason they refused to accept the Messias is that they couldn't bear to give up their professional status as God's special representatives. They didn't like our Lord's healing blind men on the Sabbath, because this offended their professional ethics.

What our Lord seems to require first of all from all of us is this relinquishing of the professional attitude. This is real poverty of spirit. Where would we be if Matthew had insisted on remaining a professional tax-gatherer? If Peter, Andrew, James and John had stuck to professional fishing? If she had been a professional Carmelite and nothing more, would the Little Flower ever have stumbled into her "little way"? A really great professional is always an amateur at heart. If Einstein had been a professional in the narrow sense, could he ever have formulated relativity, using concepts no more complicated than had been available to Adam? Amateurs are always discovering wonders that were "there all the time."

Being an amateur is essentially taking the mystical approach to all problems. It's the capacity to stand outside academic formulas and head straight for one's object because that object is irresistibly attractive. Amateur is a word which means "lover," and Christ calls only amateurs.

There are such things as professional housewives. Phenenna was one, certainly. Some of them pride themselves on being professional cooks, or professional mothers. Some are professional girdle-makers. But the amateur housewife is the perennial jack-of-all-trades who takes good care to be master of none. Everything she does must be done for pure love, not professional reasons, the way a dedicated amateur passionately pursues his hobby. Every saint is an amateur. St. Perpetua was an amateur martyr as well as an amateur writer. She tells us one of her worst trials was her pagan father, who kept trying to get her to deny her faith and save her life.

"I'd tell him, for instance," she says, "'do you see that jug, or that little pot, whatever it is, lying over there on the ground?' "'Yes,' he said. 'I see it:

"And I told him, 'Can you call it by any other name than what it is?'" [Please note the subtle difference between her question and Juliet's: the difference between martyrdom and suicide ... She doesn't say, like Juliet, "Does it matter what you call it?" but, "Can you call it anything but what it is?" What a delicate but important point!]

"And he said, 'No.'

"'Well then, I can't be called anything but what I am—a Christian!'

"Then my father, infuriated at the sound of this word, threw himself on me as if to scratch out my eyes."

Eventually Hilarianus, the Procurator before whom she appeared to be judged, found it his unpleasant duty to command her to sacrifice to the gods. She says he told her, "'Have pity on your father's gray hairs and your infant son. Come on, sacrifice to the health of the emperors!'

"'No,' I answered.

"'You're a Christian?' he asked.

"And I answered, 'I'm a Christian.'

"My father kept trying to make me recant. Hilarianus ordered him thrown out; he was even struck with a rod. The blow to my father hurt me as if I had been struck myself: I felt so sorry for his miserable old age.

"Then Hilarianus pronounced sentence on all of us and condemned us to the beasts. Happy as larks, we went down to the dungeon."

At the pace of a hen, no doubt.

Among her companions was St. Felicity. As a special insult to their sex, these two young mothers were thrown to a wild cow in the games. This refinement of contempt, actually contrary to arena custom, was rather lost on Perpetua, for she was in ecstasy during the entire onslaught. She was eventually dispatched by a gladiator, who had to slit her throat. He hated to do it, we are told, but she steadied his hand!

She had concluded her writing on the previous day with this wonderful sentence:

"This is what I did up to the day of the contest; as to the contest itself, let anybody who cares to write about that!"

Well, luckily for us, somebody did. And guess who it was! Tertullian!

See? I knew he'd come in handy.

OTHER BOOKS BY SOLANGE HERTZ:

On The Contrary

Beyond Politics

Utopia Nowhere

The Star-Spangled Heresy: Americanism

Apostasy in America

Sin Revisited

The Thought of Their Heart

Searcher of Majesty

ABOUT THE AUTHOR:

An established writer before the Second Vatican Council, Solange Hertz wrote for most Catholic periodicals and had five books to her credit, one a selection of the Catholic Literary Foundation. When she refused to adjust her theology to the new "Spirit of Vatican II," her manuscripts almost overnight became unacceptable to her former editors. After a series of articles on feminine spiritual for the old *Triumph* magazine, she continued speaking for tradition by successfully producing on her own, *The Thought of His Heart*, and *Sin Revisited*.

In 1973 she began writing the *Big Rock Papers*, published privately throughout the next decade and the source of the highly acclaimed *Star Spangled Heresy: Americanism*, published in 1992. Currently her articles can be found in *The Remnant*, and abroad in *Apropos*, *Christian Order* and *Action Familiale et Scolaire*. Mrs. Hertz is universally regarded as one of traditional Catholicism's foremost contemporary writers and lecturers.

Made in the
USA
Columbia, SC